Crystallization-Study
of
Daniel
and
Zechariah

Volume One

Witness Lee

The Holy Word for Morning Revival

Living Stream Ministry
Anaheim, CA • www.lsm.org

First Edition, January 2013.

ISBN 978-0-7363-6415-7

Published by

Living Stream Ministry
2431 W. La Palma Ave., Anaheim, CA 92801 U.S.A.
P. O. Box 2121, Anaheim, CA 92814 U.S.A.

Printed in the United States of America

13 14 15 16 / 5 4 3 2 1

2012 Winter Training

CRYSTALLIZATION-STUDY OF DANIEL AND ZECHARIAH

Contents

Preface

1. This book is intended as an aid to believers in developing a daily time of morning revival with the Lord in His word. At the same time, it provides a limited review of the winter training held December 24-29, 2012, in Anaheim, California, on the "Crystallization-study of Daniel and Zechariah." Through intimate contact with the Lord in His word, the believers can be constituted with life and truth and thereby equipped to prophesy in the meetings of the church unto the building up of the Body of Christ.

2. The entire content of this book is taken from *Crystallization-study Outlines: Daniel, Zechariah,* the text and footnotes of the Recovery Version of the Bible, selections from the writings of Witness Lee and Watchman Nee, and *Hymns,* all of which are published by Living Stream Ministry.

3. The book is divided into weeks. One training message is covered per week. Each week presents first the message outline, followed by six daily portions, a hymn, and then some space for writing. The training outline has been divided into days, corresponding to the six daily portions. Each daily portion covers certain points and begins with a section entitled "Morning Nourishment." This section contains selected verses and a short reading that can provide rich spiritual nourishment through intimate fellowship with the Lord. The "Morning Nourishment" is followed by a section entitled "Today's Reading," a longer portion of ministry related to the day's main points. Each day's portion concludes with a short list of references for further reading and some space for the saints to make notes concerning their spiritual inspiration, enlightenment, and enjoyment to serve as a reminder of what they have received of the Lord that day.

4. The space provided at the end of each week is for composing a short prophecy. This prophecy can be composed by considering all of our daily notes, the "harvest" of our inspirations during the week, and preparing a main point with

v

some sub-points to be spoken in the church meetings for the organic building up of the Body of Christ.

5. Following the last week in this volume, we have provided reading schedules for both the Old and New Testaments in the Recovery Version with footnotes. These schedules are arranged so that one can read through both the Old and New Testaments of the Recovery Version with footnotes in two years.

6. As a practical aid to the saints' feeding on the Word throughout the day, we have provided verse cards at the end of the volume, which correspond to each day's Scripture reading. These may be cut out and carried along as a source of spiritual enlightenment and nourishment in the saints' daily lives.

7. *Crystallization-study Outlines: Daniel, Zechariah* was compiled by Living Stream Ministry from the writings of Witness Lee and Watchman Nee. The outlines, footnotes, and cross-references in the Recovery Version of the Bible are by Witness Lee. All of the other references cited in this publication are from the published ministry of Witness Lee and Watchman Nee.

Winter Training
(December 24-29, 2012)

CRYSTALLIZATION-STUDY OF DANIEL, ZECHARIAH

Banners:

We need a vision to see that the excellent Christ,
the centrality and universality of God's economy,
is the precious and preeminent One in God's move,
that as the Son of Man in ascension
He has received dominion and a kingdom, and
that His coming will terminate human government
and bring in the eternal kingdom of God.

The overcomers as the shining stars
are a duplication of Christ as the living Star,
and they are the messengers of the churches,
those who are one with Christ as the Messenger of God
and who possess the present Christ
as the living and fresh message
sent by God to His people.

Christ is everything for God's building,
and as the engraved stone with seven eyes,
the topstone of grace,
He is now transfusing what He is
and what He has accomplished into our being
so that, by becoming the same as He is
in life and nature but not in the Godhead,
we may be His reproduction
for the building of the temple of God.

In His heavenly ministry
Christ was designated to be a kingly High Priest
according to the order of Melchizedek
to minister Himself as the processed Triune God
into us in order to be our daily life supply
and enjoyment for our nourishment, refreshment,
sustenance, comfort, and strengthening,
so that we may be saved to the uttermost for
the building up of the church as the temple of God.

The Rule of the Heavens,
the Economy of God,
and the Excellent Christ
as the Precious and Preeminent One
in God's Move

Scripture Reading: Dan. 2:35, 44; 4:17, 34-35; 7:13-14;
9:24-25; 10:4-9; Rev. 11:15

Day 1   I. The central thought of Daniel is that the
ruling of the heavens by the God of the heavens over all the human government on earth
matches God's eternal economy for Christ to
terminate the old creation for the germination of the new creation and to smash and
crush the aggregate of human government
and establish the eternal kingdom of God
(2:37, 44; 4:17, 26; Rev. 11:15).

II. The Most High is the Ruler over the kingdom
of men and gives it to whomever He wills
(Dan. 4:17):

A. The book of Daniel shows that all the kings and
kingdoms of the world are under God's administration (7:9-12; 2:34-35):

1. All human government from Nimrod to Antichrist has been and will continue to be under
the ruling of the heavens by the God of the
heavens (7:8, 24-26).

2. God will rule over the world, produce a situation for Israel to be His elect, gain the church
to be His mysterious people, and have all
nations to be the peoples of the eternal kingdom of God; if we see this, we will know where
we are, and we will know the meaning of our
human life (2:34-35, 45; Eph. 5:27; Rev. 11:15).

B. God caused Nebuchadnezzar to know that he
was nothing and that the mighty God, the Ruler
over the kingdom of men, the One who gives the

kingdom to whomever He wills, is everything (Dan. 4:34-37).

Day 2   C. We need to see a vision of the throne of God as the center of God's administration (Rev. 4:2; 5:1; Ezek. 1:26b):

  1. God on the throne is behind the scene, ruling over everyone and everything (Isa. 6:1; 1 Kings 22:19).

  2. We need to "come to know that the heavens do rule" (Dan. 4:26b).

III. **We need to see God's economy as it is revealed in the book of Daniel:**

  A. Christ is the centrality and universality of God's economy; in His economy, in His plan with His arrangement, God desires to make Christ the centrality and universality of His move on earth (2:35; Col. 1:15-27; Eph. 1:10).

Day 3   B. The book of Daniel covers five main points concerning Christ:

  1. The death of Christ was all-inclusive, comprising every item in the universe (9:24-26):

    a. Christ's greatest achievement in His first appearing was to terminate the whole creation by His death (Rom. 6:6).

    b. In the universe Christ's death with His resurrection is a great landmark of the ages; in His resurrection Christ became the life-giving Spirit to germinate some of those in the old creation to be the new creation (1 Cor. 15:45b; 1 Pet. 1:3; 2 Cor. 5:17).

  2. There is the need of Christ's second coming to clear up the universe physically and materially; in particular, there is the need of Christ's second coming to terminate human government (Dan. 2:34-35, 44-45).

  3. Daniel 7:13-14 reveals that now Christ as the Son of Man is before the throne of God to receive dominion and a kingdom; He is making all the preparations to come back to rule over

the world with God's dominion (Rev. 11:15).

    4. Christ is the Companion of God's suffering people (Dan. 3:23-25).

    5. Daniel 10:4-9 reveals Christ in His excellency.

  C. Christ becomes the centrality and universality of God's elect through their environment; as God's elect, we need Christ to be wrought into us as our centrality and universality (Gal. 1:16; 4:19; Eph. 3:17a; Rom. 8:28).

Day 4 **IV. The excellent Christ, the centrality and universality of God's economy, is the precious and preeminent One in God's move (Dan. 10:4-9):**

  A. The excellent Christ, who appeared to Daniel in His preciousness, has many wonderful characteristics:

    1. Christ appeared as a Priest in His humanity, signified by the linen robe, to care for His chosen people in their captivity (v. 5a; Exo. 28:31-35).

    2. Christ appeared in His kingship in His divinity, signified by the girdle of gold, for ruling over all the peoples (Dan. 10:5b).

    3. For His people's appreciation Christ appeared in His preciousness and dignity, as signified by His body being like beryl; the Hebrew word for *beryl* could refer to a bluish-green or yellow precious stone, signifying that Christ in His embodiment is divine (yellow), full of life (green), and heavenly (blue) (v. 6a).

    4. Christ appeared in His brightness for shining over the people, as signified by His face being like the appearance of lightning, and in His enlightening sight for searching and judging, as signified by His eyes being like torches of fire (v. 6b-c).

    5. Christ appeared in the gleam of His work and move, as signified by His arms and His feet being like the gleam of polished bronze (v. 6d).

Day 5
&
Day 6

    6. Christ appeared in His strong speaking for judging people, as signified by the sound of His words being like the sound of a multitude (v. 6e).

    7. As a man, such a Christ is precious, valuable, complete, and perfect (cf. Rev. 1:13-16).

B. God's intention in His administration is to give Christ the preeminence in all things, to cause Christ to have the first place in everything (Col. 1:15, 18):

    1. The entire world situation is under the rule of the heavens by the God of the heavens to match His economy for Christ (Dan. 7:9-10; 4:34-35):

        a. In His economy, in His plan with His arrangement, God desires to make Christ the centrality and universality of His move on earth (2:34-35).

        b. In 2:35 the stone refers to Christ as the centrality, and the mountain refers to Christ as the universality.

    2. For Christ to have the preeminence in all things, God needs a people; apart from God's having a people, there is no way for Christ to be made preeminent (Col. 1:18; 3:10-11; Eph. 3:21; 1 Tim. 3:15):

        a. Christ must have the first place, the preeminence, in our personal universe (Col. 3:17; 1 Cor. 10:31).

        b. Today Christ, the preeminent One, must be the centrality and universality in our church life, family life, and daily life (Col. 3:17; 1 Cor. 10:31).

        c. Under His heavenly rule God is using the environment to make Christ the centrality (the first) and the universality (everything) to us (Rom. 8:28; Col. 1:18, 27; 3:4, 10-11).

    3. As those who have been chosen by God to be His people for Christ's preeminence, we are

under God's heavenly rule (Dan. 4:26b; Matt.
4:17; 5:3):

a. The purpose of the heavenly ruling is to
complete God's elect so that Christ may be
preeminent, that He may be the first—
the centrality—and everything—the
universality (Dan. 2:35; Col. 1:18; 3:4,
10-11).

b. We all need to learn that this universe is
under God's administration and that God's
intention in His administration is to make
Christ preeminent, to cause Him to have
the first place in everything (1:18).

Morning Nourishment

Dan. **This matter is by the decree of the watchers, and**
4:17 **the decision is a command of the holy ones, to the**
intent that the living may know that the Most High
is the Ruler over the kingdom of men and gives it
to whomever He wills...
26 **...Your kingdom will be assured to you after you**
have come to know that the heavens do rule.

The central thought of Daniel is that the ruling of the heavens
(4:26) by the God of the heavens (2:37, 44) over all the human government on earth matches God's eternal economy for Christ to
terminate the old creation for the germination of the new creation
and to smash and crush the aggregate of human government and
establish the eternal kingdom of God.

The God of the heavens rules over all human government.
Human government began with Nimrod in Genesis 10. Prior to
Genesis 10 there were no human nations; instead, there was
only mankind as a whole without established nations. Nations
began to be established by Nimrod, who built Babel, a prefigure
of Babylon (Gen. 10:8-10). Human government will conclude
with the coming Antichrist, who will be the last Caesar of the
Roman Empire. All human government from Nimrod to Antichrist has been and will continue to be under the ruling of the
heavens by the God of the heavens. (*Life-study of Daniel,* pp. 4-5)

Today's Reading

In God's economy, Christ has terminated the old creation for
the germination of the new creation in His resurrection through
His death. This was achieved in His first coming. In God's economy, Christ, by His upcoming appearing, will also smash and
crush the aggregate of human government throughout the history of mankind and will establish the eternal kingdom of God.
All of these matters have been and will be intrinsically involved
with Israel, either positively or negatively.

The book of Daniel shows us that all the kings and kingdoms
of the world are under God's administration. Consider the

situation of the Babylonian Empire under Nebuchadnezzar.
First,...[as] a co-regent [with his father] he destroyed the city of
Jerusalem in 606 B.C. Then about 604 B.C. he became king and
reigned until 561 B.C. Eventually he was replaced by his son
and then by his grandson, Belshazzar, whose debauchery in Daniel 5 was an insult to God and who was slain in 538 B.C. At that
time the Babylonian Empire came to an end, and Darius the
Mede received the kingdom at the age of sixty-two. Darius was a
subordinate king to Cyrus (see Daniel 8). In 536 B.C. Cyrus issued
the decree that released the captives of Israel to return to Judah,
thus ending the seventy years which God had apportioned for the
Israelites to remain in Babylon. Therefore, God used the Babylonian Empire for the purpose of carrying His corrupted and
defeated elect into captivity. After the seventy years of their captivity, God caused the Medes and the Persians to become one for
the purpose of ending the Babylonian Empire and of releasing
His people from their captivity in Babylon. This is an illustration
of how all kings and kingdoms are under God's administration.

Nebuchadnezzar was one with Satan [Isa. 14]. Concerning
Cyrus, on the contrary, Isaiah says that God delighted in him and
even made him a shepherd to care for His people. In the first year
of his reign, Cyrus proclaimed the return of God's people to Judah
(Ezra 1:1-4). He also arranged for the vessels of the house of God which
Nebuchadnezzar had brought to Babylon to be returned to Jerusalem. Thus, Cyrus is presented in a very positive way. Nevertheless, he
was still part of the great image,...a part of the human government
which will consummate in Antichrist, who will fight against God
directly. This exposes how evil the human government is.

[Daniel 4:31 says,] "To you it is spoken, King Nebuchadnezzar: The
kingdom has passed on from you." God would teach him to know
that he was nothing and the mighty God, the Ruler over the kingdom of men, the One who gives the kingdom of men to whomever
He wills, is everything. (*Life-study of Daniel,* pp. 5, 82-83, 35-36)

Further Reading: Life-study of Daniel, msgs. 1, 6

Enlightenment and inspiration: _____

_____

_____

_____

Morning Nourishment

Rev. **Immediately I was in spirit; and behold, there was**
4:2 **a throne set in heaven, and upon the throne *there***
     ***was* One sitting.**

11:15 **And the seventh angel trumpeted; and there were**
       loud voices in heaven, saying, The kingdom of the
       world has become the *kingdom* of our Lord and of
       His Christ, and He will reign forever and ever.

God's plan is hidden in heaven. When God finds a man on earth after His heart, heaven is opened to him. It was opened to Jacob (Gen. 28:12-17), to Ezekiel (Ezek. 1:1), to Jesus (Matt. 3:16), to Stephen (Acts 7:56), and to Peter (Acts 10:11). In Revelation 4:1 and in 19:11, it is opened to John, the writer of this book, and it will be opened to all believers in the Lord in eternity (John 1:51). (*Life-study of Revelation,* p. 213)

Today's Reading

In heaven, there is firstly a throne, and the book of Revelation is focused upon it [cf. 4:2]. Beginning with chapter four, this book unveils God's universal administration. The throne of God in Revelation is the center of God's administration. While the throne in the Epistles is the throne of grace from which we receive mercy and find grace (Heb. 4:16), the throne here is the throne of judgment from which the world receives judgment. This is God's throne in heaven. The whole universe, especially the earth, is under this throne. Whatever Satan does in the air and whatever man does on earth is under God's throne in heaven. Today, man may do anything he likes, but the throne of God in heaven is still the authority over all men and all things. No one can do anything, and nothing can happen outside of the rule of God's throne. Apparently, this throne is invisible and is not realized by man, but actually it is behind the scene ruling over everyone and everything. In God's time and for the fulfillment of God's purpose, the appropriate judgment always comes out of this throne to mankind and upon the things transpiring on earth. In the book of

Revelation, the consummate issue comes from the completion of the execution of God's judgment. This judgment proceeds from the throne and clears up the confusion both in heaven and on earth caused by Satan's rebellion and man's fall. (*Life-study of Revelation*, pp. 213-214)

In Daniel 4:26 Daniel said to Nebuchadnezzar, "Your kingdom will be assured to you after you have come to know that the heavens do rule." It is the heavens that rule, not Nebuchadnezzar or Cyrus or Alexander the Great or illness or turmoil or rebellion. The earth is under the rule of a heavenly administration. The heavens rule for us, and Christ is for us.

The books of Daniel and Revelation unveil God's economy. According to His economy, God will rule over the world, produce a situation for Israel to be His elect, gain the church to be His mysterious people, and have all the nations to be the peoples in the eternal kingdom of God. If we see this, we will know where we are, and we will know the meaning of our human life.

Although the book of Daniel is short, it has many points, it speaks of many events and persons, and it contains many spiritual lessons for us. But above, behind, and within all these things, there is something else, and this is God's economy. Of course, the expression *God's economy* is not found in Daniel; neither is it found anywhere else in the Old Testament. Nevertheless, God's economy is revealed in this book. We all need to see God's economy in the book of Daniel. If we see this vision of God's economy, our whole being will be changed....Christ is the centrality and universality of God's economy, and God's economy is for Christ to be the centrality and universality in God's move. This is what we must see in our reading of the book of Daniel. The various spiritual lessons and the historical details covered in this book are very good, but they are secondary. What is primary is that in His economy, in His plan with His arrangement, God desires to make Christ the centrality and universality of His move on earth. (*Life-study of Daniel*, pp. 77, 58, 73)

Further Reading: Life-study of Revelation, msgs. 17, 19

Enlightenment and inspiration: _____

_____

_____

_____

Morning Nourishment

1 Pet. Blessed be the God and Father of our Lord Jesus
1:3 Christ, who according to His great mercy has
regenerated us unto a living hope through the res-
urrection of Jesus Christ from the dead.
Gal. My children, with whom I travail again in birth
4:19 until Christ is formed in you.

Concerning...Christ [as the centrality and universality of God's move on earth,] the book of Daniel covers five main points: the death of Christ, the upcoming appearing of Christ, Christ as the Son of Man who comes to the throne of God to receive dominion and a kingdom, Christ as the Companion of the suffering witnesses of God, and the excellency of Christ. (*Life-study of Daniel*, pp. 73-74)

Today's Reading

The first point is Christ's death, Christ's crucifixion. Regarding this, Daniel 9:26 says, "After the sixty-two weeks Messiah will be cut off and will have nothing." This word is simple, but it is rich in its implications. The death of Christ was all-inclusive, comprising every item in the universe. The main item terminated by the death of Christ was the old creation. After God's work in creation, Satan came in to corrupt, poison, devastate, and ruin God's creation. As a result, the entire old creation became not only corrupt but corruption. Yet God still uses that corrupted creation in producing a new creation through Christ's death and resurrection.

Christ's greatest achievement in His first appearing was to terminate the whole creation by His death. In this termination, however, there is something rising up, that is, Christ's resurrection. In His resurrection Christ became a life-giving Spirit (1 Cor. 15:45b) to enliven, to germinate, to regenerate, some of those in the old creation to be the new creation. This new creation begins with the believers as God's sons and Christ's members as the constituents of His Body. This Body will grow and eventually consummate in the New Jerusalem (Rev. 21—22), the total aggregate and consummation of God's new creation. This is all involved in Christ's first coming with His death and resurrection.

Even though the old creation has been terminated, outwardly the world is still the same. Hence, there is the need for Christ's second coming to clear up the entire universe physically and materially. In particular, there is the need...to terminate human government. According to Daniel 2:35 and 44, Christ will come as the stone cut out without hands to crush the great human image from the toes to the head. In His coming as such a stone, He will crush Antichrist with the ten toes. However, He will not come by Himself; He will come with His bride (Rev. 19:11, 14).

Daniel 7:13-14 reveals that now Christ as the Son of Man is before the throne of God to receive dominion and a kingdom. He is making all the preparations to come back to rule over the entire world with God's kingdom....While Christ is preparing to come back with the kingdom, He is also the Companion of God's suffering people (3:23-25). Because of the wrong government, God's people are in the "furnace," yet Christ is with them....Furthermore, 10:4-9 reveals Christ in His excellency. Every part of Christ is excellent and precious. He is the excellent One in the whole universe. This excellent One is the centrality and universality of God's economy.

The book of Daniel also reveals that it is through their environment that Christ becomes the centrality and universality of God's elect. Through the nations as the environment, in the coming days God will eventually make Christ the centrality and universality of Israel. The principle is the same with us today. In this present age of mystery, which is not revealed in Daniel, God is using the environment to make Christ the centrality and universality to us. We are not simple. On the one hand, we, the believers in Christ, are God's elect; on the other hand, we are parts of the old creation, including such negative things as the beasts described in Daniel 7. As God's elect, we need Christ to be wrought into us as our centrality and universality. (*Life-study of Daniel,* pp. 74-76)

Further Reading: Life-study of Daniel, msg. 12; *The Centrality and Universality of Christ,* ch. 2

Enlightenment and inspiration: _____

_____

_____

_____

Morning Nourishment

Dan. I lifted up my eyes and I looked, and there was a cer-
10:5-6 tain man, clothed in linen, whose loins were girded
with the fine gold of Uphaz. His body also was like
beryl, His face like the appearance of lightning, His
eyes like torches of fire, His arms and His feet like
the gleam of polished bronze, and the sound of His
words like the sound of a multitude.

Daniel, a man on the earth, set his heart to understand the
future, the destiny, of Israel (Dan. 10:2-3, 12). This he did for
twenty-one days....After those twenty-one days, Daniel saw a
particular vision in verses 4 through 9. The excellent Christ, the
centrality and universality of God's move on the earth, appeared
to Daniel for his appreciation, consolation, encouragement,
expectation, and stabilization. (*Life-study of Daniel,* p. 93)

Today's Reading

God revealed to [Daniel] the excellent man....Daniel may not
have known that this man was the Messiah, but I believe that Daniel understood that this One was the Lord as a man. That man was
not only Jehovah but Jehovah becoming a man.

In the universe there is the fact that the Triune God became a
man. This is revealed in Matthew and Luke. But in Genesis 18 when
three persons came to Abraham, there was one among the three
who was Jesus. He came as a man to visit Abraham. In Daniel 10 this
man appeared to Daniel. When He appeared as a man to Abraham,
He was an ordinary man with no particular characteristics. However, He appeared to Daniel with many wonderful characteristics.

First, the excellent Christ appeared in His priesthood for taking care of His chosen people (v. 5a). His priesthood is signified by
the linen robe. He appeared to Daniel not wearing armor for
fighting but dressed in a linen robe, the Old Testament priestly
garment....The fact that Christ is clothed in linen signifies that
His humanity is His priestly robe. At the time of Daniel 10, Christ
Himself, God's centrality and universality, was a Priest taking
care of the children of Israel in captivity. He is a Priest in His

humanity taking care of God's captive people.

Second, Christ appeared to Daniel in His kingship (signified by the golden girdle) for ruling over all the peoples [v. 5b]....A girdle is for strengthening. Christ's kingship is signified not by linen but by gold. His priesthood is human, whereas His kingship is divine.

Furthermore, for His people's appreciation Christ appeared also in His preciousness and dignity as signified by His body being like beryl (v. 6a). The Hebrew word for *beryl* here is not easily translated. Darby uses the term *chrysolite*. The Hebrew word could refer to a bluish-green or yellow precious stone. This signifies that Christ in His embodiment is divine (yellow), full of life (green), and heavenly (blue)....Furthermore, Christ appeared in His brightness for shining over the people. His brightness is signified by His face being like the appearance of lightning (v. 6b)....Christ's enlightening sight for searching and judging is signified by His eyes being like torches of fire (v. 6c)....Christ also appeared in His gleam in His work and moves, tested by people and testing people. His gleam in His work and moves is signified by His arms and His feet being like the gleam of polished bronze (v. 6d). In typology, bronze signifies God's judgment, which makes people bright. God's judgment is a kind of trial. Christ was judged, tried, by God, and God's trial and judgment made Him bright like polished bronze. Such a Christ is the One who has been tested by others and who also tests others....Finally, Christ appeared to Daniel in His strong speaking for judging people. His strong speaking is signified by the sound of His words being like the sound of a multitude (v. 6e).

The Christ whom Daniel saw was such a One. He is precious, valuable, complete, and perfect. As a man He is the very centrality and universality of God's move to carry out His economy. He is so precious, bright, shining, enlightening, and testing. As the Priest He is taking care of us, and as the King He is ruling over us. How wonderful He is! (*Life-study of Daniel*, pp. 93-95)

Further Reading: Life-study of Daniel, msg. 15; Life-study of Colossians, msg. 5

Enlightenment and inspiration: _____

_____

_____

_____

Morning Nourishment

Dan. I watched until thrones were set, and the Ancient of
7:9-10 Days sat down. His clothing was like white snow, and
the hair of His head was like pure wool; His throne
was flames of fire, its wheels, burning fire. A stream
of fire issued forth and came out from before Him.
Thousands of thousands ministered to Him, and ten
thousands of ten thousands stood before Him. The
court of judgment sat, and the books were opened.

The entire world situation is under the rule of the heavens by
the God of the heavens, to match His economy for Christ. Today
the world situation, especially in Europe and the countries
around the Mediterranean Sea, has been balanced and brought
into a condition which is ready for Christ's return. He is at the
door and the time is near. As we see this situation, we must wake
up and realize that the world is not for us. We are for Christ, and
every day we must prepare ourselves to meet Him. Then we will
receive a reward from Him.

The book of Daniel covers some very important matters. First, this
book covers the history of Israel....It also covers human government from
Nimrod to Antichrist. Because Israel and human government are
for Christ, the book of Daniel also reveals certain aspects of Christ.
Christ is the center and the circumference, the centrality and the
universality, of God's move. (*Life-study of Daniel,* p. 5)

Today's Reading

We need to see that Christ is the preeminent and all-inclusive
One, the centrality and universality of God. The book of Colossians
reveals that Christ is preeminent, that He has the first place in
everything. Both in the first creation and in the new creation
Christ occupies the first place. In 1:15 we are told that Christ is the
"Firstborn of all creation," and in 1:18, that He is the "Firstborn
from the dead." The new creation of God is by resurrection. For
Christ to be preeminent in the new creation means that He is the
first in resurrection. He is the first both in creation and in resurrection. This means that He is the first in the old creation, the

universe, and in the new creation, the church. The universe is the environment in which the church exists as the Body of Christ to express Christ in full. Christ is not only first in the church, the Body, but also first in the environment, the universe. This means that He is first in everything.

Colossians 1:19 says, "For in Him all the fullness was pleased to dwell." What is the fullness spoken of in this verse? Many would answer that it is the fullness of the Godhead. Although this is correct, here Paul does not modify the word fullness by a phrase such as "of the Godhead" or "of God." He simply says that all the fullness was pleased, was happy, to dwell in Christ. There is something in this universe known as the fullness, and this fullness is pleased to dwell in the preeminent, all-inclusive Christ.

He must have the first place in the environment and in the church. He is the preeminent One.

He is also the all-inclusive One. Christ is the reality of all the positive things in the universe. If we know the Bible and God's economy, we shall realize that Christ is the heavens, the earth, the sun, life, light, the star, trees, flowers, water, air, and food. The material things are pictures of what He is to us. Furthermore, Christ is all the divine attributes, such as power, holiness, righteousness, kindness, and love. He is also the human virtues, such as humility and patience. Moreover, He is the church and every member of the church, God's building and every stone in the building.

As the all-inclusive One, Christ is the centrality and universality of God....Christ is the center and the circumference of God's purpose. Christ is both the centrality and universality of God's purpose. He is the hub and also the rim. In other words, Christ is all. Again I say that this is not pantheism. It is simply a statement of the fact that Christ is both the center and the circumference of God's economy....In God's economy Christ is everything. (*Life-study of Colossians,* pp. 41-44)

Further Reading: The Centrality and Universality of Christ, ch. 1;
   Life-study of Revelation, msg. 18

Enlightenment and inspiration: _____

_____

_____

_____

Morning Nourishment

Dan. Then the iron, the clay, the bronze, the silver, and the
2:35 gold were crushed all at once, and they became like
chaff....And the stone that struck the image became
a great mountain and filled the whole earth.

44 ...The God of the heavens will raise up a kingdom
which will never be destroyed;...it will crush and put
an end to all these kingdoms; and it will stand forever.

Whereas Daniel 2 speaks of Christ coming as a stone cut out
without hands, Revelation 19 speaks of Christ coming as the One
who has His bride as His army. Christ is God coming down to fight
against rebellious mankind, and mankind is represented by one
man who is one with Satan—Antichrist. The very God is embodied
in Christ; Christ is with His bride, the overcomers; and Antichrist
is one with Satan and one with the ten kings and their armies.
These two parties—Christ and Antichrist—will fight. Man will
fight against God directly (Rev. 19:19-21; 17:14). The most evil persons on earth will be gathered by Antichrist to one place; that is,
the grapes will be gathered together into the winepress (19:15;
14:19-20). Then Christ will come not only to crush the ten toes but
also to tread the winepress. This will be Christ's crushing of the human government. (*Life-study of Daniel*, p. 75)

Today's Reading

After crushing the human government, God will have cleared
up the entire universe. The old creation will be gone, and the human government will become chaff blown away by the wind. Then
the corporate Christ, Christ with His overcomers, will become a
great mountain to fill the whole earth, making the whole earth
God's kingdom (Dan. 2:35, 44). (*Life-study of Daniel*, p. 75)

The great mountain [in verse 35] signifies the eternal kingdom
of God, which will fill the whole earth forever (v. 44; 7:13-14)....
Thus the great human image will be replaced with the eternal
kingdom of God on earth (Rev. 11:15-17). The increase of the stone
into a great mountain signifies the increase of Christ (cf. John
3:29-30). The church is Christ's increase in life, but the eternal

kingdom of God is Christ's increase in administration (Mark 4:26-29). Hence, Christ is not only the church but also the kingdom of God (1 Cor. 12:12; Luke 17:21). As the stone, Christ is the centrality of God's move, and as the mountain, He is the universality. Hence, He is the all-inclusive One, the One who fills all in all (Eph. 1:23). (Dan. 2:35, footnote 3)

For Christ to be the preeminent One, God needs a people. Apart from God's having a people, there is no way for Christ to be made preeminent. As those who have been chosen by God to be His people for Christ's preeminence, we are under God's heavenly rule. Concerning this, the principle is the same both in the Old Testament and in the New Testament. Under God's heavenly rule, everything is working together for our good (Rom. 8:28). This is especially true of the things in our personal universe. Our universe includes ourselves, our families, and the church. In our universe many things happen day by day for the purpose of making Christ preeminent. We need to realize this and be submissive to God's heavenly rule.

We are under God's heavenly rule for Christ. The purpose of the heavenly ruling is to complete God's elect so that Christ may be preeminent, that He may be the first—the centrality—and everything—the universality. Because the heavens rule, Christ is with us in all our situations. When we are sick, He is with us. When we are in turmoil, He is with us. I can testify that we can enjoy His presence in the midst of turmoil and rebellion.

We all need to learn three things: that this universe is under God's administration; that God's intention in His administration is to make Christ preeminent, to cause Him to have the first place in everything; and that for the accomplishment of God's intention, we, His people, His elect, must give Him the best coordination and cooperation. Through our coordination and cooperation, God will consummate His eternal intention to make Christ preeminent through the rule of the heavens. (*Life-study of Daniel,* pp. 77-78)

Further Reading: Life-study of Daniel, msgs. 5, 13, 17

Enlightenment and inspiration: _____

_____

_____

Hymns, #495

1   Christ is God's centrality
And His universality;
He is God's delight and joy
Throughout all eternity.

2   He's th' embodiment of God,
In Him all God's fulness dwells;
His unique supremacy
And His Godhead none excels.

3   All God's purpose is for Him,
That He might be all in all;
All the things in heav'n and earth
With Himself are made withal.

4   All creation is for Christ,
Everything was made by Him;
'Tis by Him all things subsist,
He's the hub and He's the rim.

5   In redemption He is all,
All through Him is reconciled;
By His blood all things with God
Now in peace are domiciled.

6   He the great beginning is,
And the Church's living Head;
He her life and content too,
And the firstborn from the dead.

7   In God's Kingdom He's the King,
All the pow'r to Him is giv'n;
In His glory He shall rule
Over all in earth and heav'n.

8   In new heaven and new earth
Center of all things He'll be,
For the Godhead and for man
Throughout all eternity.

9   God intends in everything
Christ should have preeminence,
And that such a Christ of all
We should now experience.

Composition for prophecy with main point and sub-points: _____

_____
_____
_____
_____
_____
_____
_____
_____
_____
_____
_____
_____
_____
_____
_____
_____
_____
_____
_____
_____
_____
_____
_____
_____
_____
_____
_____
_____
_____
_____
_____
_____
_____
_____

A Pattern of a Person Used by God to Turn the Age

Scripture Reading: Dan. 1:8-9; 2:17-19; 6:10; 9:23; 10:11, 19

Day 1

I. **The Lord used Daniel and his companions—Hananiah, Mishael, and Azariah—to turn the age of the captivity of God's people to the age of their return to the land of Immanuel for the building of God's house and God's city for God's expression and authority (Dan. 1:1-21; 2:17; Isa. 8:8):**

A. Every time God wants to make a dispensational move, an age-turning move, He must obtain His dispensational instrument; we must be those who have dispensational value to God (Rev. 12:5-11; 1:20; Dan. 12:3; Matt. 13:43).

B. Christ as the unique Overcomer includes all the overcomers; the unique Overcomer dwells in our spirit to make us His overcomers (John 14:30; Dan. 2:34-35; Rev. 19:7-21; 1 John 5:4, 18-19; Rev. 3:21).

C. We need to consider what we are doing to bring in the next age; this is a special time, so there is the need of special Christians to do a special work (Matt. 16:18; Rev. 19:7; 1 Cor. 1:9; Rev. 2:4-7; Col. 1:18b; John 17:21; 1 Cor. 14:4b; Eph. 4:16; Col. 2:19).

D. An overcomer works according to the principle of the Body; the principle of the Body annuls sectarianism and individualism (1 Cor. 12:12; Phil. 1:19).

E. In God's sight an overcomer is a "man of preciousness," even "preciousness itself" (Dan. 10:11, 19; 9:23).

F. The Lord needs to raise up men who will turn the age for the recovery of God's expression and authority; among fallen mankind God's expression is torn down, and His authority is denied; Daniel and his companions truly allowed God to be expressed through them and were truly under God's authority (Gen. 1:26; Rev. 4:3a; 21:11, 18a, 24; 22:5).

Day 2

II. **Daniel had companions with whom he was absolutely consecrated to God and separated**

unto God from an age that follows Satan (Dan.
1:4-8; 5:12, 22; 6:10):

A. All those who are used by God to turn the age must
be Nazarites—voluntarily consecrated ones who are
sanctified absolutely and ultimately to God (Num.
6:1-8, 22-27; Psa. 110:3; Luke 9:62; Phil. 3:13-14).

B. Although Daniel and his companions were still
very young, they stood up as an anti-testimony,
similar to the way that Antipas did in the church
in Pergamos (Rev. 2:13).

Day 3

C. We need to flee youthful lusts and pursue Christ
in the Body and for the Body with God-given companions, "with those who call on the Lord out of a
pure heart" (2 Tim. 2:22; 3:1-5; Eccl. 4:9-12):

1. According to the divine principle, the proper
representation of the Body is always by those
who are matched with others; this matching is
determined entirely by God's arrangement, not
by man's maneuvering (Neh. 1:1; 8:2; 1 Cor. 1:1;
Exo. 4:14b-16; Phil. 2:19-22; Luke 10:1; Acts
13:1-3; 1 Thes. 1:1).

2. An overcomer lives in the Body and works
according to the principle of the Body in the
blending life of the entire Body of Christ;
whoever cannot be blended with others will
be disqualified by the age (Rom. 12:4-5; 1 Cor.
12:12, 15, 20, 25).

D. One of the subjective signs of a called one (seen
with Moses) is the sign of the water becoming
blood (Exo. 4:9); this means that in the eyes of God
all the earthly supply and worldly enjoyment (the
water of the Nile) are nothing but death (blood).

E. If we are going to live a holy life for the church life,
we must care for our diet, which is a matter of life
or death (Gen. 2:9, 17; Dan. 1:8-9; John 6:57; Matt.
4:4; Rev. 2:17).

Day 4   **III. Daniel joined himself to God's desire through
God's Word (Dan. 9:1-4; Deut. 17:18-20; 2 Tim.
3:16-17; Eph. 6:17-18; Psa. 119:11, 24):**

A. Daniel was not only a person who read God's Word regularly but also a person who was joined to God's Word:

1. When he read from the book of Jeremiah that God had ordained seventy years of captivity for the Israelites and that after seventy years God would turn back to bless them, he immediately fasted and prayed; as soon as he touched God's desire through the Word, he immediately joined himself to that desire (Dan. 9:2-3).

2. After he read the book of Leviticus, he could no longer eat the unclean food (Dan. 1:8-21); after he read the book of Jeremiah, he could not help but fast and pray for the restoration of God's people (29:10-14).

3. Whenever we find out God's desire from His Word, we must immediately join ourselves to that desire (cf. Psa. 119:11, 15-16, 133, 140).

4. The Bible should affect our living, and we should be joined to the Bible (cf. 2 Cor. 6:14-18).

5. To be an anti-testimony, one must read God's Word and touch God's desire from His Word; God's living word works in us to separate us from the world and move us out of our divisive self into the oneness of the Triune God (John 17:17, 21; Eph. 5:26).

B. Daily we need to practice coming to the Word to have the Triune God as truth infused into us according to the following life principles:

1. We must open our entire being to the Lord for the inner shining of the divine light and the supplying of the divine life; the one who experiences the greatest amount of transformation is the one who is absolutely open to the Lord (Psa. 119:105; Prov. 20:27; Psa. 139:23-24).

2. We must seek the Lord with all our heart (119:2; Mark 12:30).

3. We must deal with anything that separates

us from the Lord (Acts 24:16; 2 Tim. 1:3a;
1 John 1:9; cf. Ezek. 1:22, 26).

4. We must humble ourselves before the Lord,
putting aside our self-confidence and self-
assurance and looking to Him for His mercy
and grace (Isa. 66:1-2; 1 Pet. 5:5).

5. We must exercise our spirit to pray over and
with God's Word and exercise our whole being
to muse on His Word as the condensation of
God's light in order to receive the life supply
and the divine watering (Eph. 6:17-18; 5:26;
Psa. 119:15-16, 25, 50, 105, 130).

6. When we experience the enlightenment, the
life supply, and the watering, we shall have
other blessings through the Word: restoration
(19:7a), deliverance (119:41, 170), strength (v. 28),
comfort (v. 76), nourishment (v. 103), upholding (v. 117), and safeguard (v. 114).

Day 5   IV. **Daniel was a man of prayer with an excellent
spirit, a man fearing God, honoring God, exalt-
ing God, and living under God's rule in the reality
of the kingdom of the heavens, the ruling of the
heavens (Dan. 6:10; 9:1-4, 17; 5:12, 14; 6:3; 5:22-23;
4:25-26, 32):**

A. Fearing God means wanting God, desiring single-
heartedly to keep His will, being fully submissive
to Him, wanting nothing of ourselves, walking not
according to our will, seeing not ourselves, and
seeing God's greatness alone (5:22-23; Psa. 86:11;
Isa. 11:2).

B. To honor God is to live and walk by the Spirit for
Christ's exaltation in order to honor others by
ministering the Spirit to them (Judg. 9:9; Phil.
1:19-21a; 2 Cor. 3:6).

C. To live under God's rule is to be filled with His
ruling presence of righteousness, holiness, and
glory for the carrying out of His eternal covenant in
dispensing Himself into us to make us the wise ex-
hibition of all that He is (Gen. 9:8-17; Ezek. 1:26-28;

Rev. 4:3; 21:18-20; 1 Cor. 1:30; Eph. 3:10-11).

D. Prayer in the Spirit through the exercise of our spirit fills us with and brings us under God's ruling presence for the carrying out of His economy (Rev. 4:1-3; Eph. 6:17-18):

1. The highest expression of a man who cooperates with God is in prayer; God carries out His economy on earth through His faithful channels of prayer (Matt. 26:41; Acts 6:4; Eph. 6:18; Col. 4:2).

2. Prayer is the lifeline in the Lord's recovery; the more Satan tries to frustrate our prayer, the more we should pray (Dan. 6:10, cf. vv. 4-9).

3. Daniel was a person living before God; he depended on prayer to do what man could not do, and he depended on prayer to understand what man could not understand (2:17-19; 9:1-4; 10:1-3, 11-13).

4. Daniel's prayer was totally for God and not for himself; through prayer he afforded God the highest cooperation (9:2b; Jer. 25:11; Dan. 9:17; 1 Kings 8:48).

5. Because Daniel was a man of prayer, he was acknowledged by God, qualified to be used by God, and capable of speaking forth the mystery of God (cf. Acts 6:4).

6. Daniel's prayer reached the highest peak; he asked God to do something for Himself; he prayed, "Now hear, O our God, the prayer of Your servant and his supplications, and cause Your face to shine upon Your sanctuary that has been desolated, for the Lord's sake" (Dan. 9:17).

7. Only a person like Daniel, who prayed to God single-heartedly, can be used by Him to turn the age.

Day 6 V. **Daniel was a self-sacrificing person with the spirit of martyrdom (6:10-11):**

A. Daniel prayed at the risk of his life; the intention of the chief ministers and satraps was to destroy Daniel, but the intention of Satan, who was behind them, was to cut off the channel of prayer that God was using for the carrying out of His economy (vv. 4-24).

B. Daniel's companions did not care for their own lives; when they were commanded by the king to bow down to a golden image, they said, "O Nebuchadnezzar,...our God whom we serve is able to deliver us from the blazing furnace of fire, and He will deliver us out of your hand....But if He does not,...we will not serve your gods nor worship the golden image that you have set up" (3:16-18).

C. Everyone whom God uses to turn the age is afraid of only one thing, that is, of offending God and losing His presence (2 Cor. 5:9-10; cf. Psa. 51:11; Josh. 7:4).

D. If we contact the Christ typified by the vine and experience His sacrificing life, He will energize us to live a life of sacrifice, producing happiness for God and for others (Judg. 9:13; Matt. 9:17; Rom. 12:1; Eph. 5:2; 2 Cor. 1:24):

1. In ourselves we are not able to live a life of sacrifice, for our life is a natural life, a selfish life (Job 2:4; Matt. 16:25).

2. Christ's love of affection constrains us to live and to die to Him (2 Cor. 5:14-15; Rom. 14:7-9).

3. Christ's love makes the believers martyrs for Him (Rev. 2:10; 12:11; Rom. 8:35-37).

4. If we experience Christ as the wine-producing vine, we will be filled with joy in the Lord (John 15:11; Acts 5:41; 13:52; Phil. 3:1a; 4:4; Psa. 43:4).

5. By experiencing Christ as the wine-producing vine and by being filled with Him as the new wine, we may become a drink offering in Him and with Him to be poured out for God's satisfaction and for God's building (Gen. 35:14; Exo. 29:40-41; Phil. 2:17; 2 Tim. 4:6).

Morning Nourishment

Rev. And she brought forth a son, a man-child, who is to
12:5 shepherd all the nations with an iron rod; and her
child was caught up to God and to His throne.
10-11 ...Now has come...the kingdom of our God and the
authority of His Christ, for the accuser of our brothers has been cast down....And they overcame him...

According to the Bible, the seed of the woman will bruise the
head of the enemy. The seed of the woman in Genesis 3 primarily
refers to the Lord Jesus, but the overcomers also have a part in
this seed. The seed of the woman includes the church, especially
the overcomers. Even though the Lord bruised Satan's head, he is
still at work. The fulfillment of the seed of the woman bruising
Satan can be seen in the man-child in Revelation 12. The only
Overcomer includes all the overcomers (vv. 10-11).

When God changes His attitude towards a certain matter, He
makes a dispensational move. Every dispensational move brings
in God's new way. His most important dispensational move is in
Revelation 12. He wants to end this age and bring in the age of the
kingdom....How can He bring this age to a close and bring in
another? He must have His dispensational instrument. This is
what God wants to do today. (Watchman Nee, *The Glorious
Church,* p. 153)

Today's Reading

The rapture of the man-child brings an end to the church age
and introduces the kingdom age. The man-child enables God to
move. If there is not a man-child and a rapture, God cannot make a
dispensational move. We should never forget that God can be limited. He waits for man in all of His moves. God's binding in heaven
is based on our binding on earth; God's loosing in heaven is based
on our loosing on earth. Everything depends on the church.

It is God's desire that created beings would deal with fallen created beings. According to His purpose, the whole church should
deal with Satan; however, the church has failed. Therefore, there is
the need for the overcomers to rise up. God's purpose is fulfilled in

the overcomers because they work with Him. We can see the principle of the overcomers throughout the Word of God. God always lays hold of a group of overcomers to make a dispensational move.

The Lord has two works on earth: redemption and building the church. The church is built on "this rock" (Matt. 16:18). The apostles were the first to stand on this rock. Even though they were weak in the flesh, their spirits were not weak....They were a dispensational instrument....The apostles and disciples waited for ten days, praying in Jerusalem. They might have said, "We have a great work to do after these days; we should rest now." Instead, they prayed. There were one hundred and twenty, but where were the others who had followed the Lord? Clearly, not everyone will work with God. These one hundred and twenty were overcomers.

Are we at the end of the age? If we are, the kingdom will soon begin. If a dispensational move is near, then God needs an instrument. General work is no longer adequate. The children of God lack a vision; they do not see the seriousness and intensity of the situation. *Now* is a matter of dispensation. Just being a good servant of the Lord is no longer good enough; this is not of great use to God....This is a special time, so there is the need of special Christians to do a special work.

Today God is waiting for the man-child. Only the rapture can precipitate the events in Revelation 12:10. God has an order, and He works according to that order. His eyes have left the church; they are now on the kingdom. An overcomer works according to the principle of the Body. The principle of the Body annuls sectarianism and individualism.

Of all the dispensational moves, the man-child is the greatest because it removes man's power and the devil's power, and it brings in the kingdom. We live in the most privileged time; we can do the most for God. *Light will show us the way, but strength and power will enable us to walk the road. A great price must be paid in order to be used now. (The Glorious Church, pp. 153-157)*

Further Reading: The Glorious Church, pp. 153-157

Enlightenment and inspiration: _____

_____

_____

_____

Morning Nourishment

Dan. But Daniel set his heart not to defile himself with
1:8 the king's choice provision and with the wine that the
king drank...

Rev. I know where you dwell, where Satan's throne is; and
2:13 you hold fast My name and have not denied My faith,
even in the days of Antipas, My witness, My faithful
one, who was killed among you, where Satan dwells.

How did God use Daniel to turn that age? There is an important principle with Daniel as also with Samuel. It is voluntary consecration. Samuel was a Nazarite. A Nazarite was a person who consecrated himself voluntarily (Num. 6)....Apparently Daniel was not a Nazarite. Actually he was, because a Nazarite was a person who did not drink any wine or strong drink. What is the meaning of not drinking wine or strong drink? It means not to enjoy any pleasures of this life. This is the principle with Daniel.

Why did Daniel drink neither wine nor strong drink, nor partake of the king's diet? It is because all these things were related to idols. What the king of Babylon drank, as well as his meat and grains, must have been offered to the idols. At least those meals were not clean according to the ordinances on cleanliness in Leviticus 11; it was defiled food. Daniel said, "I will not be defiled by that food. The young people of the world may participate in it. But I will not have a part in it." (*Men Who Turn the Age*, p. 12)

Today's Reading

Daniel refused everything that men enjoyed and boasted of. He refused everything that would offer him some position in the world. He was a voluntarily consecrated one....A little spiritual pursuit or a little godly living before the Lord is not enough to be used by the Lord to turn the age. All those who are used by the Lord to turn the age must be Nazarites; they must be voluntarily consecrated ones. I believe by now all of us know what voluntary consecration means. It means that when everyone else on earth seeks after the world and enjoys the world, I separate myself from it. This separation is a voluntary consecration. The Bible records that in those days the king of Babylon chose a group of young men from different races to stand before him. The opportunity of being chosen was something beyond one's dream because the king would give them good food and drink for three years so that they would be fair and fat in the flesh to stand before him in the palace. Many yearned for such opportunity but were not able to have it. Yet Daniel and his three companions vowed, saying, "We forsake such opportunity. We will not enjoy the food and drink here. We cannot be the same as other people. We must take another stand. Other people do not have God and are not for God, but we are for God."

They expressed God this way because they submitted themselves to His authority. While the whole earth denied God's authority, they acknowledged God's authority. While the whole earth had men as kings, they had God as their King.

Although Daniel and his three friends were still very young, they stood up to be an anti-testimony. This anti-testimony is a separation. As soon as they stood up, there was clearly a separation from the world....When we read Daniel 1, we must grasp the meaning of this picture. These men did not follow the tide of Babylon at all. They were the separated ones. They could not eat what others could eat. They could not drink what others could drink. They could not do what others could do. They were clearly different from others in everything. (*Men Who Turn the Age,* pp. 12-14, 19)

In Greek *Antipas* means "against all." Antipas, a faithful witness of the Lord, stood against all that the worldly church brought in and practiced. Hence, he became a martyr of the Lord. In Greek the word for *martyr* is the same as that for *witness.* Antipas, as an anti-witness, bore an anti-testimony, a testimony against anything that deviated from the testimony of Jesus. It must have been through his anti-testimony that in his days the church in Pergamos still held fast the Lord's name and did not deny the proper Christian faith. (Rev. 2:13, footnote 3)

Further Reading: Men Who Turn the Age, ch. 1

Enlightenment and inspiration: _____

_____

_____

_____

Morning Nourishment

Exo. ...Is there not Aaron your brother the Levite?...
4:14-16 And even now he is coming out to meet you; and
when he sees you, he will be glad in his heart. And you
shall speak to him and put the words in his mouth,
and I will be with your mouth and with his mouth, and
will teach you what you shall do. And he shall speak
for you to the people, and he shall be as a mouth for
you, and you shall be as God to him.

I believe that deep in His heart the Lord wanted Aaron to be a
match for Moses. When the Lord Jesus sent out His disciples, He
sent them out two by two (Luke 10:1), that is, in the principle of
two as a testimony. To be alone is to be individualistic, but to be
sent forth with another is to be sent according to the principle of
the Body. Thus, to have Aaron as a match for Moses was according
to the divine principle.

Although this was according to God's principle, God did not simply tell Moses that he needed Aaron to match him. But if we read
this portion carefully, we shall see that this was already in God's
heart....The Lord was hoping that Moses would realize his need for
someone to match him. Although the Lord was ready to do this, He
did not point this out to Moses until he himself became conscious of
his need. The Lord is very wise. He may be willing to do a certain
thing for us, but He often will not do anything until we realize our
need. This principle has an application among us in the church life.
Although you may realize that I need a certain thing, it is better for
you not to tell me. Instead, you should wait until I realize my need.
(*Life-study of Exodus,* pp. 97-98)

Today's Reading

In keeping with the divine principle, the Lord would not
allow His servant to be individualistic. Moses needed Aaron.
Hence, Aaron's presence was not accidental. God had prepared
him as a match for Moses.

This principle of matching applies today. If you have been

called by the Lord, you need to realize your need for someone to match you....When the apostle Paul came out to serve the Lord, he did not behave individualistically. He always had others to match him. This is proved by the opening verse of 1 Corinthians: "Paul, a called apostle of Christ Jesus through the will of God, and Sosthenes the brother." When Paul wrote this Epistle, neither Timothy nor Barnabas was present. Therefore, Paul took Sosthenes as a match; he took a brother whose name we hardly know in order to keep the principle.

To act individualistically in the Lord's service is not according to the divine principle. Today, in the New Testament economy, to be individualistic is to violate the principle of the Body. We should not behave individualistically; rather, we should move and act according to the principle of corporateness, always having at least one other member to match us. The more members we have to match us, the better it is. The Body cannot be represented by individuals. According to the divine principle, the proper representation of the Body is always by those members who are matched with others....A matching one binds us and restricts us. For this reason, it is difficult to be matched with others.

According to the record, Aaron might have been more capable than Moses in the matter of speaking; Aaron might have been more eloquent than Moses. However, Aaron was not to take this as an occasion to be proud. He could only do a certain amount, for God did not give him so much as far as position was concerned. In fact, Exodus 4:16 says that Moses was to be as God to Aaron. From the match of Moses and Aaron we all can learn the importance of knowing where we are. The place we occupy in a matching relationship depends entirely on the Lord's arrangement. The Lord called Moses and He prepared Aaron to match him. There was no place for human maneuvering. Everything was according to the divine economy, the divine arrangement. (*Life-study of Exodus,* pp. 99-101, 103)

Further Reading: Life-study of Exodus, msgs. 8-10

Enlightenment and inspiration: _____

_____

_____

Morning Nourishment

Dan. In the first year of his reign I, Daniel, understood by
9:2-3 means of the Scriptures the number of the years,
which came as the word of Jehovah to Jeremiah
the prophet, for the completion of the desolations of
Jerusalem, *that is,* seventy years. So I set my face
toward the Lord God to seek *Him* in prayer and
supplications with fasting and sackcloth and ashes.

Daniel was not only a person who read God's Word regularly,
but a person who was joined to God's Word....We should believe
that he refused the food and drink of the king of Babylon because
he had read the five books of Moses....[In them] he must have
found out that God's people cannot partake of any food that has
touched the idols. Since he read these commandments and therefore
knew God's desire, he accepted them and applied them to himself.
Hence, he was not a person separate from the Scripture.

When he read from the book of Jeremiah that God had ordained seventy years of captivity for the Israelites, and that after
seventy years God would turn back to bless them, he immediately
fasted and prayed. He did not read the Scripture in a dead way. As
soon as he touched God's desire through the Word, he immediately
joined himself to that desire.

This was the way he read the Bible. This was why he could be
touched by every word, by the light, and by the teaching in the
Bible. After he read the book of Leviticus, he could no longer eat
the unclean food. After he read the book of Jeremiah, he could not
help but fast and pray for the restoration of God's people. Which-
ever point he read, he joined himself to that point....Whenever we
find out God's desire, we must immediately join ourselves to that
desire. (*Men Who Turn the Age,* pp. 21-22)

Today's Reading

If we want to receive blessing from the Word of God, we must
first deal with our heart and turn to the Lord absolutely and with
our whole heart. We also need to deal with anything in our heart
that is negative or that causes separation between us and the Lord.

The Bible demands that we humble ourselves and put aside our self-confidence and self-assurance....If we do not receive the Lord's mercy, something within us unconsciously may continue to cover us and keep us from the Lord's Word.

As the embodiment of God, the unique light, the Word of God is a shining light. This light is actually God Himself in the Word. Because the Word is the condensation of the divine light, we enter into an atmosphere of light whenever we come to the Word. This is like entering into a lighted room. When we are in a lighted room, we do not simply receive light, but we are in a realm of light.

When we come to the Word of God, we need to open...[and] use our whole being, our body, soul, and spirit. We use our eyes to read the words and our mouth to sound out the words. We also use our mind, the main part of the soul, to understand what we read. We may need to use lexicons, concordances, and different versions and translations. God created us with a mind, and we need to use it in understanding the Word of God. The study of the Bible also requires the exercise of our emotion to love the Word and the exercise of our will to take God's way in His Word. This exercise of the mind, emotion, and will is the exercise of the soul. But we also need to exercise our spirit. Primarily this is to pray so that our inner man may be strengthened. If we use our whole being in contacting the Word, we shall receive light and life supply.

When we experience the enlightenment, the life supply, and the watering, we shall have other blessings through the Word: restoration (Psa. 19:7a), deliverance (119:41, 170), strength (v. 28), comfort (v. 76), nourishment (v. 103), upholding (v. 117), and safeguard. The reference to strength in verse 28 refers not to something doctrinal, but to something that fills us inwardly and energizes us. This must denote an organic element, for only something organic can enter our being to strengthen us. The fact that the Word of God strengthens us indicates that it imparts an organic element into us. *(Life-study of Exodus,* pp. 692-694, 696, 699, 702)

Further Reading: Life-study of Exodus, msg. 59

Enlightenment and inspiration: _____

_____

_____

_____

Morning Nourishment

Dan. ...(In his upper room [Daniel] had windows open
6:10   toward Jerusalem) and three times daily he knelt
       on his knees and prayed and gave thanks before
       his God, because he had *always* done so previously.

9:17   And now hear, O our God, the prayer of Your ser-
       vant and his supplications, and cause Your face to
       shine upon Your sanctuary that has been deso-
       lated, for the Lord's sake.

Fearing God means wanting God, desiring single-heartedly
to keep His will, being fully submissive to Him, wanting nothing of ourselves, walking not according to our will, seeing not
ourselves, and seeing God's greatness alone. (*The Collected
Works of Watchman Nee,* vol. 9, p. 349)

Daniel...was a man who was always praying. His prayers
were not at all common. His prayers were prayers that turned the
age. Every time he encountered some crucial matter, he prayed
before God....He believed in prayer because he believed in God
and not in himself. (*Men Who Turn the Age*, pp. 23-24)

Today's Reading

[In Daniel 2] before the king of Babylon called for Daniel, he
declared that if none of the magicians or learned ones in Babylon under him could explain the dream, he would destroy them
all. Among those who were to be killed were Daniel and his three
friends. I fully believe that Daniel would have told his three friends
to pray with him. There they afforded God the highest cooperation;
they gave God the highest coordination. In their single-hearted
prayer, God revealed to Daniel the dream....This shows that
Daniel was a person living before God; he depended on prayer to
do what man could not do, and he depended on prayer to understand what man could not understand. He was a person who
cooperated with God in prayer.

We should believe that Daniel would not have seen the dream

nor understood its meaning if he had not prayed....Through prayer he afforded God the highest cooperation.

The book of Daniel records Daniel as a person who could pray.... His prayer touched God's heart and was able to fulfill God's plan. Satan purposely wanted to deal with his prayer and to destroy his prayer. Chapter 6 especially shows us that Satan wanted to damage this praying person through the men under Satan. At least he tried to destroy his prayer and to render him unable to pray.

Satan's subtle strategy was to utilize the men around King Darius to deal with Daniel, to stop Daniel from praying, and eventually to ensnare Daniel, the man of prayer. How did Daniel respond to this? He still prayed as usual and was not at all threatened by it. The Bible is very clear: "Three times daily he knelt on his knees and prayed and gave thanks before his God, because he had always done so previously" (Dan. 6:10). Nothing could stop Daniel's praying. If Daniel had not prayed, Daniel would have failed. As long as Satan could destroy and stop Daniel's prayer, Satan would win. Hence, Daniel's prayer was like a stronghold on a battlefield.

We must realize that it was this prayer of Daniel that resulted in God being manifested as the living God. With Daniel, God truly manifested Himself as the living God. And this manifestation of God was due to Daniel's prayer.

[In 9:17] Daniel's prayer reached the highest peak. He asked God to do something for Himself....I hope that we would circle the words "for the Lord's sake." We can see that his prayer was totally for God and not for himself. It seems as if he was saying to God, "My supplication here today is not for myself but for You. Even though I am asking You to do something, it is not for myself, but for You." This was a very special prayer; it was also the highest prayer. Our prayers are ninety-nine and nine tenths percent for ourselves. Very few of them are for God. Only a person like Daniel, who prayed to God single-heartedly, can be used by Him to turn the age. (*Men Who Turn the Age,* pp. 25-28)

Further Reading: Men Who Turn the Age, ch. 2

Enlightenment and inspiration: _____

_____

_____

_____

Morning Nourishment

Dan. ...**Our God whom we serve is able to deliver us from**
3:17-18 **the blazing furnace of fire, and He will deliver *us* out of**
your hand, O king. But if *He does* not, let it be known
to you, O king, that we will not serve your gods nor
worship the golden image that you have set up.

Daniel was a person who would sacrifice himself to be martyred.... The book of Daniel shows us that a person who is under God's hand and who is used by Him to turn the age is a self-sacrificing person. Every incident and fact shows us that he was a person who did not care for his own life. For example, when he chose to eat vegetables only, he did not necessarily have the assurance that he would be strong. If the more he ate, the slimmer he became, he would be killed by the king of Babylon. Yet he cared neither for life nor for death. He knew that the unclean food, the food sacrificed to idols, could not enter into his mouth, that he would not be defiled, and that he would keep God's word. Because of this word, he was willing to lose even his life. (*Men Who Turn the Age*, p. 28)

Today's Reading

[In Daniel 6] King Darius decreed that within thirty days none in the kingdom could make petition of God or men. But Daniel still prayed. Even if he would be thrown into the den of lions, he would still pray. Humanly speaking, he truly had the spirit of martyrdom.

All those who are afraid of what might happen to them, who are afraid of things that come from one direction or another, of this and of that, cannot be used by God to turn the age....Everyone whom God uses to turn the age...is only afraid of one thing, that is, to offend God and to lose His presence. Anyone who hides, withdraws, withers, and changes his mind when confronted with difficulties is not of much use in God's hands. God cannot use cowards. All those whom God uses to turn the age are bold ones. They are not bold in a wild or natural way, but bold because of their fear of God and their courage to confront difficulties.

Daniel and his three friends...did not care for their own lives at all. Listen to the words of Daniel's three friends. How resolute and majestic they were!…They said, "O Nebuchadnezzar,…our God whom we serve is able to deliver us from the blazing furnace of fire, and He will deliver us out of your hand.…But if He does not,…we will not serve your gods nor worship the golden image that you have set up" (3:16-18).…The three of them would rather be bound and cast into a fiery furnace than to submit to the king. If they had been cowardly and afraid of death, surely they could not have testified for God at all that day and could not have been used by God to turn the age. (*Men Who Turn the Age,* pp. 28-29)

The most happy person is the most unselfish one. The most selfish people are always the most miserable.…The sacrificing one is the happy one. How can we sacrifice? We have no energy to sacrifice, for our life is a natural life, a selfish life. Only the life of Christ is a life of sacrifice. If you contact this Christ and experience His sacrificing life, He will energize you, He will strengthen you to sacrifice for God and for others. Then you will be the most happy person; you will be drunken with happiness. This is the experience of Christ as the vine tree. By this experience you will become a vine to others. All those who contact you will be happy with you, and you will bring cheer to God.

What must be done to the grapes to make them wine? They must be pressed. To make God and others happy, you must be pressed.…The grapes must be pressed to bring cheer to God and man. You too must be pressed. The more you drink the wine of Christ, the more you will realize that you must be pressed. (*The All-inclusive Christ,* p. 59)

Christ's love of affection constrains us to live and to die for Him (2 Cor. 5:14-15; Rom. 14:7-9).…Christ's love makes the believers martyrs for Him (Rev. 2:10; 12:11; Rom. 8:35-37).

Quite often I would not do some things, not merely because they are not right or because I fear God but because I love Him. I would say, "Lord Jesus, I love You, so I cannot do this." (*The Overcomers,* pp. 22, 31)

Further Reading: The All-inclusive Christ, ch. 5; *The Overcomers,* ch. 2

Enlightenment and inspiration: _____

_____

_____

_____

Hymns, #894

1 Will you be an overcomer?
  Christ is calling now!
 Will you then be such a follower,
  Though you know not how?

  Will you be an overcomer?
   Will you make this choice?
  Christ is calling, Christ is calling,
   Listen to His voice!

2 Will you be an overcomer?
  To the Lord be drawn!
 Keep the "first love," never leave it,
  Till the break of dawn.

3 Will you be an overcomer?
  On His life depend!
 Dare to suffer persecution,
  Faithful to the end.

4 Will you be an overcomer?
  Testimony bear!
 Keep away from false religion,
  "Hidden manna" share.

5 Will you be an overcomer,
  Simple, real, and pure?
 Overcome all evil mixture,
  Ruling pow'r secure.

6 Will you be an overcomer?
  Trust the living Lord!
 Keep your "garments" from the deadness,
  Win the life-reward.

7 Will you be an overcomer?
  Never lukewarm be,
 Ne'er content with what you've gotten,
  More you need to see.

8 Will you be an overcomer?
  Christ is calling still!
 Will you now be loyal to Him,
  His demand fulfill.

Composition for prophecy with main point and sub-points: _____

_____

_____

_____

_____

_____

_____

_____

_____

_____

_____

_____

_____

_____

_____

_____

_____

_____

_____

_____

_____

_____

_____

_____

_____

_____

_____

_____

_____

_____

_____

_____

_____

_____

_____

_____

The Vision of the Great Image—
the Controlling Vision in the Book of Daniel

Scripture Reading: Dan. 2

Day 1   I. The vision of the great image and its destiny in Daniel 2 is a vision of "what will happen in the last days" (v. 28).

II. The vision of the great image in Daniel 2 is the controlling vision in the book of Daniel:

A. This great image signifies the aggregate of human government throughout human history, from the beginning of human government at Babel (Babylon) in the land of Shinar (Gen. 10:8-10; 11:1-9), as signified by the head of the image, to the termination of human government in human history in the Roman Empire with the ten kings, as signified by the ten toes (Dan. 2:40-44a; 7:24; Rev. 13:1; 17:12):

1. The head of gold (Dan. 2:36-38), corresponding to the first beast in 7:3-4, signifies Nebuchadnezzar, the founder and the king of Babylon.

2. The breast and the arms of silver (2:39a), corresponding to the second beast in 7:5, signify Medo-Persia.

3. The abdomen and thighs of bronze (2:39b), corresponding to the third beast in 7:6, signify Greece, including Macedonia.

4. The legs of iron and the feet partly of iron and partly of clay (2:33), corresponding to the fourth beast in 7:7-8, signify the Roman Empire with its last ten kings (2:40-44a; 7:7-11, 19-26; Rev. 17:7-13).

B. From its beginning to its termination, human government has always done three things: rebel against God, exalt man, and worship idols (Gen. 11:4, footnote 2, Recovery Version).

Day 2
&
Day 3

III. **According to the human image in Daniel 2, in the sight of God all human government is composed of four empires: the Babylonian Empire, the Medo-Persian Empire, the Macedonian-Grecian Empire, and the Roman Empire:**

A. The beginning of human government was at Babel (Babylon), which was built by Nimrod (Gen. 10:8-10), and the ending of human government will be the revived Roman Empire under Antichrist.

B. Although the form and appearance of the Roman Empire have vanished, the culture, spirit, and essence of the Roman Empire continue to exist today (Dan. 7:12).

C. At the beginning of the great tribulation (Matt. 24:21) the form and appearance of the Roman Empire will be restored under Antichrist.

D. According to the books of Daniel and Revelation, the last Caesar of the Roman Empire will be Antichrist, who will be supported by ten kings (Rev. 17:10-12).

E. Thus, the aggregate of human empires that began with Nimrod at Babel will consummate with Antichrist and the ten kings.

F. If the head of the great human image is Babylon, the entire image must also be Babylon; in the eyes of God, the entire human government from Nimrod to Antichrist is Babylon:

1. Under Antichrist, the last Caesar, the Roman Empire will be both political and religious Babylon (chs. 17—18).

2. The empire of Antichrist will be the political and physical Babylon, that is, "Babylon the Great" (18:2), whereas the Roman Catholic Church, called "MYSTERY, BABYLON THE GREAT" (17:5), will be the religious Babylon (footnote on Jer. 50:1, Recovery Version).

G. The two legs of iron signify the eastern Roman Empire and the western Roman Empire, and the feet and the toes, partly of iron and partly of clay

(Dan. 2:41-43), signify the nations in the period after
the fall of Rome and before Christ's second coming:

1. These nations are partly autocratic and partly
   democratic; the ten toes of the image signify
   the ten kings of the revived and restored Roman Empire under Antichrist (v. 44a; 7:7, 24;
   Rev. 17:12).

2. The periods of history signified by the first
   three parts of the great human image and the
   two legs have been fulfilled, but the period signified by the ten toes has not yet been fulfilled;
   it will be fulfilled at the end of the present age.

Day 4 IV. **The destiny of the great human image is to**
&   **be crushed by a stone cut out without hands**
Day 5   **(Dan. 2:34-35a, 44b-45):**

   A. This stone is Christ; through His crucifixion Christ
      was cut by God by being put to death (Zech. 3:9; Acts
      2:23), and in His resurrection (v. 24) He was cut out
      to be a stone in three aspects: the foundation stone
      and the cornerstone for the building up of the
      church (Isa. 28:16; Matt. 21:42), the stumbling stone
      to the unbelieving Jews (Isa. 8:14; Matt. 21:44a;
      Rom. 9:33), and the crushing stone to destroy the
      totality of human government (Matt. 21:44b).

   B. When Christ comes as the crushing stone, He
      will not come alone; rather, He will come with
      His overcomers, His bride, His increase, as His
      army (John 3:29-30; Rev. 17:14; 19:7-8, 11, 14).

   C. During the church age, the age of mystery, Christ
      is building up the church to be His bride (Eph.
      5:25-29); before He descends to earth, Christ will
      have a wedding, in which He will marry the over-
      comers (Rev. 19:7-9), those who have been fighting
      the battle against God's enemy for years and who
      have already overcome the evil one (cf. 12:11).

   D. After His wedding, Christ as the Husband will
      come with His newlywed bride to destroy Anti-
      christ, who with his army will fight against God
      directly (17:14; 19:19).

E. At His appearing as the God-cut stone, Christ with His overcomers—the corporate Christ—will strike the ten kings with Antichrist (vv. 11-21), thereby crushing the great image from the toes to the head (Dan. 2:35).

F. This will be Christ's universal judgment on the aggregate of human government from Antichrist back to Nimrod, thus ending the age of man's government on earth in the old creation and initiating the age of God's dominion over the entire earth in the millennium and in the new heaven and new earth for eternity.

V. **"Then the iron, the clay, the bronze, the silver, and the gold were crushed all at once, and they became like chaff from the summer threshing floors; and the wind carried them away so that no trace of them was found. And the stone that struck the image became a great mountain and filled the whole earth" (v. 35):**

A. The great mountain here signifies the eternal kingdom of God, which will fill the whole earth forever (v. 44; 7:13-14).

B. After coming to crush the aggregate of human government, the corporate Christ—Christ with His overcoming bride—will become a great mountain to fill the whole earth, making the whole earth God's kingdom; thus the great human image will be replaced with the eternal kingdom of God on earth (Rev. 11:15-17).

C. The increase of the stone into a great mountain signifies the increase of Christ (cf. John 3:29-30); the church is Christ's increase in life, but the eternal kingdom of God is Christ's increase in administration (Mark 4:26-29); hence, Christ is not only the church but also the kingdom of God (1 Cor. 12:12; Luke 17:21).

D. As the stone, Christ is the centrality of God's move, and as the mountain, He is the universality; hence, He is the all-inclusive One, the One who fills all in all (Eph. 1:23).

Day 6   **VI. We need to see what our attitude should be in the light of the vision of Christ and His overcoming bride coming as a corporate smiting stone to smash the totality of human government and becoming a great mountain, the kingdom of God, to fill the whole earth:**

A. If, as God's people, we see this controlling vision in Daniel 2, we will be kept from the world and prepared for Christ's coming.

B. Since we know that the Lord's coming is so precious, we should have a living that loves the Lord's appearing; this will cause us not to be discouraged, not to backslide, not to become weak, but to remain faithful to the end (2 Tim. 4:8; cf. John 14:21).

C. The last prayer in the Bible is "Come, Lord Jesus!" (Rev. 22:20); we should all pray such a prayer and have such a desire; the entire Bible concludes with the desire for the Lord's coming expressed as a prayer.

D. Every "today" that we have is truly the Lord's grace; therefore, as long as we have today, as long as we still have breath, we should love the Lord and His appearing, await the Lord's coming (Phil. 3:20), and always take His coming as an encouragement.

E. When the Lord comes, He will come secretly as a thief to those who love Him and will steal them away as His treasures and bring them into His presence in the heavens (Matt. 24:42-43); hence, we need to watch and be ready (25:13; 24:44).

F. To attain maturity is not an overnight matter; therefore, for His coming to set up His kingdom we must prepare ourselves, love Him, and grow in Him, that at His appearing we may be mature to be raptured and receive the reward (Heb. 6:1a; Luke 21:34-36; cf. Rev. 12:5-6, 14).

Morning Nourishment

Dan. But there is a God in the heavens who reveals myster-
2:28 ies, and He has made known to King Nebuchadnezzar
what will happen in the last days. This is your dream,
even the visions of your head upon your bed.

31-32 You, O king, were watching, and there was a single great
image. This image, large and its brightness surpassing,
stood opposite you; and its appearance was frightful.
Concerning this image, its head was of fine gold...

The vision of the great image in Daniel 2...is the controlling vision in the book of Daniel....Chapter 1 is simply an introduction, whereas chapter 2 shows us a controlling vision, a vision that is the key to understanding Daniel's visions in chapters 7 through 12.

This great image signifies the aggregate of human government throughout human history (2:31-33), from the beginning of human government in Babel (Babylon) in the land of Shinar (Gen. 10:6-12), as signified by the head, to the termination of human government in human history in the Roman Empire with the ten kings, as signified by the ten toes. From its beginning to its termination, human government has done and will continue to do three things: rebel against God, exalt man, and worship idols (Gen. 11:4, 9). (*Life-study of Daniel,* pp. 21, 23, 14)

Today's Reading

In the great human image, the head of gold, corresponding to the first beast in Daniel 7:3 and 4, signifies Nebuchadnezzar, the founder and the king of Babylon (2:36-38)....The breast and the arms of silver, corresponding to the second beast in 7:5, signify Medo-Persia (2:39a)....The abdomen and thighs of bronze, corresponding to the third beast in 7:6, signify Greece, including Macedonia (2:39b)....The legs of iron and the feet partly of iron and partly of clay, corresponding to the fourth beast in 7:7 and 8, signify the Roman Empire with its last ten kings (2:40-43).

In the Bible, according to the human image in Daniel 2, there are only four empires. In the sight of God, therefore, all of human government throughout human history is composed of four empires: the Babylonian Empire, the Medo-Persian Empire, the Macedonian-Grecian Empire, and the Roman Empire. According to the human point of view, the Grecian Empire ended with the death of Alexander the Great. However, according to God's viewpoint, this empire continued with Alexander's successors—his four generals who divided the empire into four sections—and it lasted until the beginning of the Roman Empire. Apparently the Roman Empire has also been terminated. Actually the Roman Empire continues to exist. According to the books of Daniel and Revelation, the Roman Empire will have as its last Caesar the Antichrist, with the ten kings signified by the ten toes of the great image. The Roman Empire, which began approximately thirty years before the birth of Christ, will last until the very end of the three and a half years of the great tribulation. The aggregate of human empires that began with Nimrod at Babel will consummate with the last Caesar of the Roman Empire with his ten kings. Thus, according to the Bible, we are still in the Roman Empire today.

The culture of the world is an accumulation of culture from the time of Nimrod until the present. What began with Nimrod will conclude with Antichrist. The Babylonian, Medo-Persian, and Macedonian-Grecian Empires have vanished, but their culture remains. The Medo-Persian Empire adopted aspects of Babylonian culture, and the Macedonian-Grecian Empire adopted aspects of Medo-Persian culture. In the same principle, the Roman Empire adopted many elements of Greek culture and of the cultures that preceded it. Today we are still under the influence of Roman culture, especially in the matters of law, politics, and government. In this sense, the Roman Empire continues to exist, and we are still in this empire.

In the interpretation of Nebuchadnezzar's dream in chapter 2, only the head of the great human image was called Babylon. However, if the head is Babylon, the entire image must also be Babylon. (*Life-study of Daniel,* pp. 14-16, 21)

Further Reading: Life-study of Daniel, msg. 3

Enlightenment and inspiration: _____

_____

_____

_____

Morning Nourishment

Dan.　Concerning this image, its head was of fine gold,
2:32-33　its breast and its arms of silver, its abdomen and its
　　　　thighs of bronze, its legs of iron, its feet partly of
　　　　iron and partly of clay.
7:12　And as for the rest of the beasts, their dominion
　　　　was taken away, but an extension of life was given
　　　　to them for a season and a time.

Although the dominion and authority of Babylon, Persia, and Greece were taken away, their life, that is, their culture, has been extended and still remains. As each empire was defeated, its culture was adopted by each succeeding empire. Today the world's culture is Roman, yet, being an accumulated culture, it contains the cultures of the Babylonians, Persians, and Greeks. (Dan. 7:12, footnote 1)

At the beginning of the great tribulation (Matt. 24:21) the form and appearance of the Roman Empire will be restored under Antichrist. According to the books of Daniel and Revelation, the last Caesar of the Roman Empire will be Antichrist, who will be supported by ten kings (Rev. 17:10-12 and footnotes). Thus, the aggregate of human empires that began with Nimrod at Babel will consummate with Antichrist and his ten kings. (Dan. 2:32, footnote 1)

Today's Reading

The Bible reveals that the human image seen by Nebuchadnezzar in Daniel 2 actually...[began] with Nimrod, who founded the city of Babel (Gen. 10:9-10)....Babylon has since continued through the Medo-Persian Empire, the Grecian Empire, and the Roman Empire. It will eventually include the last Caesar of the Roman Empire, Antichrist, with his ten kings, signified by the toes of the great image (Dan. 2:41-44). The book of Revelation tells us that under Antichrist, the last Caesar, the Roman Empire will be both political and religious Babylon. Revelation 18 refers to the empire of Antichrist as the political and physical Babylon, that is, "Babylon the Great" (v. 2). Furthermore, through Constantine the Great, who accepted Christianity as the state religion, the nature of Christianity was changed to become the Catholic Church, which in Revelation 17 is called "MYSTERY, BABYLON THE GREAT" (v. 5). This is the religious Babylon. Therefore,...not only Babylon itself is Babylon, but even the Roman Empire is Babylon.

According to our point of view, there are many different countries, nations, and empires. But in the eyes of God, the entire human government from Nimrod to Antichrist is Babylon. We need to consider what part of the great human image we are in today. As the result of studying the Bible and the world situation for over sixty years, I believe that today we are at the feet of the image, very close to the ten toes. The world situation, especially the situation in Europe, has been remodeled to fit in with the prophecies in the Bible. If we are clear about this, we will know where we are and what we should do. The culture, spirit, and essence of the Roman Empire continue to exist, but the form and appearance of this empire have vanished. However, the form and appearance of the Roman Empire will be restored under Antichrist. The whole earth is now ready for the restoration of the Roman Empire and the appearing of the ten toes, which will bring in Christ as the stone to crush the aggregate of human government and usher in the eternal kingdom of God upon the earth.

The four empires in Daniel 2 correspond to the four beasts in Daniel 7. In chapter 2 Nebuchadnezzar saw a great human image, but in chapter 7 Daniel saw four beasts....The head of gold (2:37-38), signifying Nebuchadnezzar, corresponds to the first beast, which "was like a lion and had the wings of an eagle" (7:3-4). The breast and arms of silver (2:32, 39a), signifying Medo-Persia, correspond to the second beast, which resembled a bear (7:5). The abdomen and thighs of bronze (2:32, 39b), signifying Greece, correspond to the third beast, which was like a leopard (7:6). The legs of iron and the feet partly of iron and partly of clay (2:40-43), signifying the Roman Empire and its last ten kings, correspond to the fourth beast, which, being different from the other beasts, had large iron teeth and ten horns (7:7-8). (*Life-study of Daniel,* pp. 21-23)

Further Reading: Life-study of Daniel, msg. 4

Enlightenment and inspiration: _____

_____

_____

_____

Morning Nourishment

Dan. ...There was a fourth beast, dreadful and frightful
7:7 and exceedingly strong;...and it was different from
all the beasts that were before it; and it had ten horns.
Rev. And the beast who was and is not, he himself is also
17:11-12 the eighth and is out of the seven....And the ten
horns which you saw are ten kings, who...receive
authority as kings for one hour with the beast.

[In Daniel 2] the two legs of iron signify the eastern Roman Empire and the western Roman Empire, and the feet and the toes, partly of iron and partly of clay (vv. 41-43), signify the nations in the period after the fall of Rome and before Christ's second coming. These nations are partly autocratic and partly democratic. The ten toes of the image signify the ten kings of the revived and restored Roman Empire under Antichrist (v. 44a; 7:7, 24; Rev. 17:12). The periods of history signified by the first three parts of the great human image and the two legs have been fulfilled, but the period signified by the ten toes has not yet been fulfilled. It will be fulfilled at the end of the present age. (Dan. 2:33, footnote 1)

The fourth beast corresponds to the legs of iron and the feet and the toes, partly of iron and partly of clay, of the great human image in 2:33, 40-43, signifying the Roman Empire, and specifically Antichrist, the last Caesar of the Roman Empire (Rev. 17:7-11).... The fourth beast was dreadful and frightful and exceedingly strong, as signified by iron. That it had large iron teeth and claws of bronze, and that it devoured, crushed, and trampled down the remainder (Dan. 7:19, 23) signify that it had great power to devour and crush nations. The beast having ten horns signifies that it had ten kings (v. 24; Rev. 17:12-13), which are the ten toes of the great human image in chapter 2. (Dan. 7:7, footnote 1)

Today's Reading

All biblical students who are familiar with prophecy know that the image illustrates the world political situation beginning with Nebuchadnezzar. The head of gold symbolizes Nebuchadnezzar, the king of Babylon, and thus the Babylonian Empire (Dan. 2:37-38). The breast and arms of silver symbolize Medo-Persia (v. 39). The belly and thighs of bronze symbolize the empire of Macedonia and Greece under Alexander the Great (v. 39). Following the Greek Empire is the Roman Empire (v. 40). It is symbolized by the two legs of iron, indicating its tremendous strength.

The four kingdoms are symbolized by gold, silver, brass, and iron. The first is gold, indicating that its beginning is more glorious. The glory reduces with each succeeding metal, yet it remains very strong. Finally, the feet of the image are part iron and part clay, signifying the nations in the period after the fall of Rome and before the second coming of Christ. These nations would be part autocracy and part democracy.

In the early part of this century, communism crept into human society. The Soviet revolution occurred in 1917. After World War II, communism took control in China. The philosophy of communism was their boast. Actually, they simply practiced dictatorship, or autocracy. Today it has been about seventy years from the time communism had its beginnings in Russia. Communism is like the iron in the feet of the image. It is strong to crush whatever stands in its way, but God has a way to weaken the iron. His way is to mix it with clay. In these days the people of eastern Europe, who are the clay, the dust, are rising up to deal with and weaken the iron of communism. Eventually, the iron cannot deal with the dust, and it becomes paralyzed, crippled. This demonstrates the fulfillment of prophecy in eastern Europe, and that we are in the iron-clay stage of the image. Millions are rising up in eastern Europe. Recently, millions rose up in Red China in a desire for freedom. As the clay rises up, the strength of the iron is weakened. (*The Organic Building Up of the Church as the Body of Christ to Be the Organism of the Processed and Dispensing Triune God,* pp. 26-27)

Further Reading: The Organic Building Up of the Church as the Body of Christ to Be the Organism of the Processed and Dispensing Triune God, pp. 24-28

Enlightenment and inspiration: _____

_____

_____

_____

Morning Nourishment

Dan. 2:34 You were watching until a stone was cut out without hands, and it struck the image at its feet of iron and clay and crushed them.

44 And in the days of those kings the God of the heavens will raise up a kingdom which will never be destroyed;...it will crush and put an end to all these kingdoms; and it will stand forever.

The destiny of the great human image is to be crushed by a stone cut out without hands, at its appearing (Dan. 2:34-35a, 44b-45; 7:13-14). This stone cut without hands is Christ. As the stone that will crush the entire human government of mankind, Christ was not cut out with human hands (as indicated by "without hands" in 2:34, 45); He was cut by God through His crucifixion and resurrection. Through His crucifixion He was cut by being put to death (Acts 2:23), and in His resurrection He was cut out to be...the cornerstone for the building up of the church and the crushing stone to destroy the totality of human government (Acts 2:24; Matt. 21:42, 44b). (*Life-study of Daniel,* p. 16)

Today's Reading

At His appearing as the stone cut out not by human hands, Christ will crush the great image from the toes to the head. This means that He will strike the ten kings with Antichrist. Revelation 19 speaks of the war between Christ and Antichrist. With Christ there will be His newly-married bride, composed of the overcomers, and with Antichrist there will be the ten kings with their armies. This war will be a fighting of the earth against the heavens, of man against God. Christ will defeat and destroy Antichrist and the ten kings.

According to Daniel 2, this will entail the crushing of the entire human image from the toes to the head.... [Verse 35a says], "Then the iron, the clay, the bronze, the silver, and the gold were crushed all at once, and they became like chaff from the summer threshing floors; and the wind carried them away so that no trace of them was found." This signifies the complete destruction of all human

government from Nimrod to Antichrist. Human government will...
be terminated by Christ at His appearing as the God-cut stone.

Christ is a stone in three aspects. First, to the believers Christ is
the foundation stone in whom they trust. Concerning this aspect of
Christ as a stone, Isaiah 28:16 says, "Indeed, I lay a stone in Zion as
a foundation, / A tested stone, / A precious cornerstone as a foundation firmly established." Second, to the unbelieving Jews Christ is
the stumbling stone (Isa. 8:14; Rom. 9:33). Regarding this aspect,
Matthew 21:44a says, "He who falls on this stone shall be broken to
pieces." Third, to the nations Christ will be the smiting stone. "On
whomever it falls, it shall crush him to powder and scatter him like
chaff" (Matt. 21:44b). (*Life-study of Daniel,* pp. 16-17)

The destiny of the great human image is to be crushed by a stone
cut out without hands (Dan. 2:34-35a, 44b-45). This stone is Christ.
Through His crucifixion Christ was cut by God by being put to
death (Zech. 3:9; Acts 2:23), and in His resurrection (Acts 2:24) He
was cut out to be a stone in three aspects: the foundation stone and
the cornerstone for the building up of the church (Isa. 28:16; Matt.
21:42), the stumbling stone to the unbelieving Jews (Isa. 8:14;
Matt. 21:44a; Rom. 9:33), and the crushing stone to destroy the totality of human government (Matt. 21:44b). (Dan. 2:34, footnote 1)

After [Christ's] wedding He will come both as the smiting stone
and as the One who will tread the winepress (Rev. 19:15; 14:19-20;
Isa. 63:2-3). Antichrist will gather a vast number of evil, rebellious
human beings around Jerusalem, thus preparing the "grapes" to
be trodden in the "winepress" by Christ. His coming will be a
great surprise, for these rebellious ones will believe neither in
Christ nor in God but only in themselves. Antichrist will even go
so far as to say that he is God (2 Thes. 2:4; Dan. 11:36), and for his
enjoyment will set up his tent between the good land and the
Mediterranean Sea (v. 45). Then Christ as the God-cut stone will
come with His bride to strike the toes of the image, destroying it
from the toes to the head. (*Life-study of Daniel,* pp. 17-18)

Further Reading: Life-study of Daniel, msg. 3

Enlightenment and inspiration: _____
_____
_____
_____

Morning Nourishment

Dan. ...And the stone that struck the image became a
2:35   great mountain and filled the whole earth.
 45   Inasmuch as you saw that out of the mountain a
       stone was cut without hands and that it crushed
       the iron, the bronze, the clay, the silver, and the
       gold, the great God has made known to the king
       what will happen afterward...

When Christ comes as the crushing stone, He will not come
alone; rather, He will come with His overcomers, His bride, His
increase, as His army (John 3:29-30; Rev. 17:14; 19:7-8, 11, 14).
During the church age, the age of mystery, Christ is building up
the church to be His bride (Eph. 5:25-29). Before He descends to
earth, Christ will have a wedding, in which He will marry
the overcomers (Rev. 19:7-9), those who have been fighting the
battle against God's enemy for years and who have already overcome the evil one (cf. Rev. 12:11). After His wedding, He as the
Husband will come with His newlywed bride to destroy Antichrist, who with his army will fight against God directly (Rev.
17:14; 19:19). (Dan. 2:34, footnote 1)

At His appearing as the God-cut stone, Christ with His overcomers—the corporate Christ—will strike the ten kings with
Antichrist (Rev. 19:11-21), thereby crushing the great image
from the toes to the head (Dan. 2:35). This will be Christ's universal judgment on the aggregate of human government from
Antichrist back to Nimrod, thus ending the age of man's government on earth in the old creation and initiating the age of God's
dominion over the entire earth in the millennium and in the new
heaven and new earth for eternity. (Dan. 2:34, footnote 2)

Today's Reading

The great human image will be replaced with a great mountain, signifying the eternal kingdom of God, which will fill the
whole earth (Dan. 2:35b, 44a). This means that after Christ
comes to crush the aggregate of human government, He will
usher in the eternal kingdom of God on earth.

This increase of the stone into a great mountain signifies the increase of Christ. The fact that Christ can increase is clearly revealed in John 3. Referring to Christ, verse 30 says, "He must increase." The increase in this verse is the bride spoken of in verse 29: "He who has the bride is the bridegroom." Christ, therefore, has an increase, and this increase is His bride. Just as Eve was the increase of Adam, the bride is the increase of Christ as the Bridegroom.

The church today is Christ's increase in life, but the eternal kingdom of God is Christ's increase in administration. In life Christ increases to become the church; in administration Christ increases to become the eternal kingdom of God. Hence, Christ is not only the church but also the kingdom of God. Both the church and the kingdom are His increase.

The parable of the seed in Mark 4:26-29 reveals how the kingdom of God is the increase of Christ. Verse 26 says, "So is the kingdom of God: as if a man cast seed on the earth." This seed is Christ as the embodiment of the divine life. According to the parable, this seed sprouts, grows, bears fruit, matures, and brings forth a harvest (vv. 27-28). From the time Christ came to sow Himself into the "soil" of humanity, He has been growing and increasing. Eventually, this increase will become the great mountain that fills the whole earth to be the eternal kingdom of God.

The word regarding Christ as the stone and the mountain in chapter 2 of Daniel reveals that Christ is the centrality and the universality of God's move. We may say that as the stone He is the centrality and that as the mountain He is the universality. The stone is Christ as the center, and the mountain is Christ as the circumference, the universality. Christ truly is the all-inclusive One. He is the stone and also the mountain; He is the church and also the kingdom. He with His increase is the great mountain that fills the whole earth. (*Life-study of Daniel,* pp. 18-19)

Further Reading: Life-study of Daniel, msg. 4

Enlightenment and inspiration: _____
_____
_____
_____

Morning Nourishment

Dan. **I watched in the night visions, and there with the**
7:13-14 **clouds of heaven One like a Son of Man was coming;**
and He came to the Ancient of Days, and they
brought Him near before Him. And to Him was given
dominion, glory, and a kingdom, that all the peoples,
nations, and languages might serve Him. His domin-
ion is an eternal dominion, which will not pass away;
and His kingdom is one that will not be destroyed.

I hope that we will all see the controlling vision in Daniel 2 and
that, in light of this vision, we will have a clear view regarding human government. In the eyes of human beings, there are different
kinds of governments, some good and others bad. But in the eyes of
God, every human government is a beast....I can testify that this
view has preserved me from the world for more than sixty years....
If, as God's people, we see this controlling vision, we will be kept
from the world and prepared for Christ's coming as the smiting
stone which will crush the aggregate of human government and
become a great mountain—the eternal kingdom of God—filling
the whole earth. (*Life-study of Daniel*, p. 24)

Today's Reading

Since we know that the Lord's second coming is so precious, we
should love the Lord's appearing (2 Tim. 4:8). The Bible concludes
with "Come, Lord Jesus!" (Rev. 22:20)....In their hearts the apostles firmly believed that the Lord would come quickly, and they also
lived a life in preparation for the Lord's second coming....Do not
think that since we are clear concerning the signs of the Lord's
coming, we can be slothful and can first love the world and then
pursue the Lord when the last week comes....We should believe
that the Lord is to be feared. In Luke 12 the Lord gave a parable
concerning a rich man who endeavored to lay up wealth for himself
so that his soul might enjoy itself and be merry. But God said to
him, "Foolish one, this night they are requiring your soul from you"
(vv. 16-20). Every "today" that we have is truly the Lord's grace.
Therefore, as long as we have today, as long as we still have breath,

we should love the Lord and His appearing, await the Lord's coming (Phil. 3:20), and always take His coming as an encouragement.

Paul said,…"I solemnly charge you before God and Christ Jesus, who is to judge the living and the dead, and by His appearing and His kingdom" [2 Tim. 4:1]. This is an exhortation…immediately before his martyrdom. He said that he had fought the good fight, he had finished the course, and he had kept the faith, and that at the judgment seat he would be awarded the crown of righteousness, which would be awarded to all those who have loved His appearing (vv. 6-8). He reminded Timothy, and also us, by the Lord's judgment and kingdom that we should have a living that loves the Lord's appearing. This will cause us not to be discouraged, not to backslide, not to become weak, but to remain faithful to the end.

When the Lord comes, He will come secretly as a thief to those who love Him, and will steal them away as His treasures and bring them into His presence in the heavens (Matt. 24:42-43). Hence, we need to watch and be ready (Matt. 25:13; 24:44). If we desire to be raptured, first we must be filled with the heavenly breath and have oil in our vessels. If we are rooted on the earth and occupied daily with the anxieties of this life and with earthly pleasures, we will not be raptured at that time. We should remember Lot's wife. Because she loved and treasured the evil world which God was going to judge and utterly destroy, she took a backward look. Thus, she became a pillar of salt and was left to suffer in a place of shame. This should be a warning to us. If we love the world, the Lord will leave us here to pass through the great tribulation that we may be put to shame until we become mature and are raptured.

To attain maturity is not an overnight matter. Therefore, for His coming we must prepare ourselves, love Him, and grow in Him, that at His appearing we may be mature to be raptured and receive the reward. (*The Up-to-date Presentation of the God-ordained Way and the Signs concerning the Coming of Christ*, pp. 67-69)

Further Reading: The Up-to-date Presentation of the God-ordained Way and the Signs concerning the Coming of Christ, ch. 7

Enlightenment and inspiration: _____

_____

_____

_____

Hymns, #947

1   God's Kingdom today is a real exercise,
     But when Christ comes to reign it will be a great prize;
     It is wisdom divine that we now may be trained
     That His plan be fulfilled and His justice maintained.

2   God's children, we're born to be kings with His Son,
     And we need to be trained that we may overcome
     And to know how to rule in His kingdom as kings,
     That His kingship thru us be expressed o'er all things.

3   Today we must learn to submit to His throne,
     How to have a strict life and His government own;
     His authority then we'll be able to share,
     O'er the nations to rule with God's Son as the heir.

4   With a life strict to self we must righteousness hold,
     Kind to others in peace, and with God joyful, bold;
     In the Kingdom's reality e'er to remain,
     For its manifestation prepared thus to reign.

5   Then Christ when He comes with the kingdom from God
     Will to us grant His kingship to share as reward;
     Thus the Lord will His righteousness thru us maintain
     And His wisdom to heavenly powers make plain.

6   For this the Apostle pressed on at all cost,
     For the Kingdom assured that he would not be lost;
     'Tis for this he charged others, Be true to the Lord,
     That the Kingdom might be unto them a reward.

7   O Lord, give us grace for Thy Kingdom to live,
     To be trained that Thou may the reward to us give;
     Make the Kingdom's reality our exercise,
     That its manifestation may be our great prize.

Composition for prophecy with main point and sub-points: _____

_____

_____

_____

_____

_____

_____

_____

_____

_____

_____

_____

_____

_____

_____

_____

_____

_____

_____

_____

_____

_____

_____

_____

_____

_____

_____

_____

_____

_____

_____

_____

_____

_____

The Vision of the Seventy Weeks and the Age of Mystery

Scripture Reading: Dan. 9:24-27; Rev. 10:7

Day 1 I. **Daniel 9:24-27 is the most precious portion in the book of Daniel; the seventy weeks in these verses are the key to understanding all the prophecies in the Bible (Dan. 7:7, 23-25; 12:7; Rev. 12:14; 13:1; 17:12):**

A. In his desperate prayer Daniel requested that God recover the Holy Land, send His people back, and rebuild the holy city; God answered him by giving him a vision of the seventy weeks (Dan. 9:2, 15-19, 24).

B. The purpose of the seventy weeks is "to close the transgression, and to make an end of sins, and to make propitiation for iniquity, and to bring in the righteousness of the ages, and to seal up vision and prophet, and to anoint the Holy of Holies" (v. 24):

1. When Christ comes at the time appointed to crush human government, the righteousness of the ages, the eternal righteousness, will be brought in; the coming kingdom age will be an age of righteousness, and in the new heaven and new earth righteousness will dwell (Isa. 32:1; 2 Pet. 3:13).

2. The sealing up of vision and prophet indicates that after the seventy weeks everything will be accomplished and fulfilled (Dan. 9:24c).

3. At the time of Daniel's prayer, the Holy of Holies was contaminated, defiled, and devastated, but when the apportioned time comes, the Holy of Holies will be properly anointed; this means that the service to God will be recovered (v. 24c).

C. The seventy weeks are divided into three parts, each week being seven years in length (vv. 25-27):
   1. First, seven weeks (forty-nine years) were apportioned from the issuing of the decree to restore and rebuild Jerusalem to the completion of the rebuilding (v. 25; Neh. 2:1-8).
   2. Second, sixty-two weeks (434 years) were apportioned from the completion of the rebuilding of Jerusalem to the cutting off (crucifixion) of the Messiah (Dan. 9:26).
   3. Third, the last week of seven years is for Antichrist to make a firm covenant with the people of Israel (v. 27).

Day 2   D. *Messiah will be cut off and will have nothing* refers to the crucifixion of Christ, which was the termination of the old creation, with the human government in the old creation, and the germination of God's new creation through the resurrection of Christ, with God's eternal kingdom as the divine administration in God's new creation; thus, the cross of Christ is the centrality and universality of God's work (v. 26; Mark 9:12; 1 Pet. 1:3; 2 Cor. 5:17; Matt. 16:19, 28).

E. There is a gap of unknown duration between the first sixty-nine weeks and the last week of the seventy weeks:
   1. This gap is the age of the church, the age of mystery, the age of grace (Eph. 3:3-11; 5:32; Col. 1:27).
   2. During this gap, the age of the church, Christ is secretly and mysteriously building up the church in the new creation to be His Body and His bride (Matt. 16:18; Eph. 5:25-32).

F. *He will make a firm covenant with the many for one week* (Dan. 9:27) refers to Antichrist, typified here by Titus, the prince mentioned in verse 26:
   1. In the middle of that week Antichrist will break the covenant and will cause the sacrifice and oblation to cease; this will be the

beginning of the great tribulation, which
will last for three and a half years (7:25;
12:7, 11a; Matt. 24:21; Rev. 11:2-3; 12:6, 14;
13:5).

  2. The fact that the temple will be devastated
and contaminated by Antichrist strongly
indicates that the temple will be rebuilt by
the Jews before the completion of the seventy weeks; this will be one of the final
signs that will take place before Christ's
return (2 Thes. 2:3-4).

Day 3 II. **"To seal up vision and prophet" (Dan. 9:24c)
is to close the age of mystery, that is, to finish
the mystery of God (Rev. 10:7; 1 Tim. 3:9):**

  A. In the dispensation from the incarnation of
Christ to the millennial kingdom—the church
age, the age of grace—everything is a mystery:

  1. The incarnation of Christ, as the beginning
of the age of mystery, is a mystery; through
the incarnation of Christ, the infinite God
was brought into the finite man (v. 16).

  2. Christ is the mystery of God (Col. 2:2):

    a. God is a mystery, and Christ, as the em-
bodiment of God to express Him, is the
mystery of God.

    b. As the mystery of God, Christ is the em-
bodiment of God; all the fullness of the
Godhead dwells in Christ bodily (v. 9).

  3. The church is the mystery of Christ (Eph.
3:4-6):

    a. Christ is a mystery, and the church, as
the Body of Christ to express Him, is the
mystery of Christ.

    b. Christ and the church as one spirit are
the great mystery (5:32; 1 Cor. 6:17).

    c. During the church age, the age of mys-
tery, Christ is building up the church to
be His bride (Matt. 16:18; Eph. 4:16; Rev.
19:7-9).

4. The kingdom of the heavens, the indwelling of Christ, and the resurrection and transfiguration of the saints are all mysteries (Matt. 13:11; Col. 1:27; 1 Cor. 15:51-53).

Day 4

B. The age of mystery is the age of faith (Heb. 11:1, 6; Rev. 10:7; 1 Tim. 3:9):

1. God's mysteries are known by faith; for this reason the age of mystery is also the age of faith (Rev. 10:7):
   a. Without faith we cannot realize God's economy, for God's economy is in faith (1 Tim. 1:4).
   b. God's requirement for us related to everything in the New Testament is faith (Rom. 1:16-17; Gal. 2:20; Eph. 3:17; Mark 11:22; Luke 18:8).

2. Faith is a substantiating ability, by which we substantiate, give substance to, the things not seen, or hoped for (Heb. 11:1):
   a. Faith assures us of the things not seen, convincing us of what we do not see; therefore, it is the evidence, the proof, of things not seen (v. 1).
   b. We do not regard, or look at, the things which are seen but the things which are not seen (2 Cor. 4:18).
   c. The Christian life is a life of things unseen, and the Lord's recovery is to recover His church from things seen to things unseen (Rom. 8:24-25; Heb. 11:27; 1 Pet. 1:8; Gal. 6:10).

C. In this age we preach the mystery of the gospel, "the proclamation of Jesus Christ, according to the revelation of the mystery" (Eph. 6:19; Rom. 16:25):

1. The gospel includes all the divine mysteries; therefore, *the mystery of the gospel* refers to the entire New Testament economy (Eph. 6:19; 1 Tim. 1:4).

2. In particular, the mystery of the gospel is Christ and the church for the fulfillment of God's eternal purpose (Eph. 5:32; 3:11).

Day 5 III. **By studying the vision of the seventy weeks in relation to God's economy, we may experience the shining of the prophetic word as a lamp conveying spiritual light in darkness, and under this shining we may receive the Lord's warning and have the proper attitude toward His coming (2 Pet. 1:19):**

A. The Lord warned us to watch and take heed to ourselves lest our hearts be weighed down with debauchery, drunkenness, and the anxieties of life, and that day come upon us suddenly as a snare (Matt. 24:42; Luke 21:34).

B. We need to be watchful at every time, beseeching that we would prevail to escape all the things which are about to happen and stand before the Son of Man (v. 36).

Day 6 C. We need to keep the word of Christ's endurance and keep the Lord's works until the end (Rev. 3:10; 2:26).

D. We should not love the present age—we should love the Lord's appearing (2 Tim. 4:10a, 8):

1. In the Bible the appearing of the Lord is typified by the morning star and by the sun (Rev. 2:28; 22:16b; Mal. 4:2):

a. His appearing as the sun is to the world; His appearing as the morning star is to the believers.

b. Before our Lord Jesus appears to the people in the world, He will first appear to those who love His appearing (2 Tim. 4:8).

2. The appearing of Christ must be a basic factor in our daily living; we must live today in the light of the Lord's appearing (Matt. 24:45-51; 25:14-30).

3. The Lord's appearing, His coming back, is a warning, an encouragement, and an incentive to us; we should love His appearing and look forward to it with earnest expectation and joy (2 Tim. 4:1-8).

Morning Nourishment

Dan. ...I, Daniel, understood by means of the Scriptures
9:2 the number of the years...for the completion of the
desolations of Jerusalem, *that is,* seventy years.
24 Seventy weeks are apportioned for your people and
for your holy city, to close the transgression, and to make
an end of sins, and to make propitiation for iniquity, and
to bring in the righteousness of the ages, and to seal up
vision and prophet, and to anoint the Holy of Holies.

Daniel 9:24-27 is the most precious portion in the entire book
of Daniel. The seventy weeks mentioned in these verses are the
key to understanding the prophecies of the Bible.

In Daniel 9:3-23 we see the way to obtain this vision—Daniel's
desperate seeking of the Lord God in prayer and supplications
with fasting....In his prayer Daniel confessed his own sins and
the sins of the kings, the chief men, and the fathers of Israel, and of
all the people of Israel (vv. 3-15, 20a)....In his prayer Daniel also
supplicated for the holy city of Jerusalem, the holy mountain of
God, and the holy people of God (vv. 16-17, 19b, 20b). This means
that he supplicated for all the interests of God on the earth, not for
his own interest....Furthermore, Daniel asked the Lord to forgive
them, not based upon their righteousness but based upon God's
great compassion (vv. 18-19a). (*Life-study of Daniel,* pp. 85-86)

Today's Reading

In Daniel 9:21-23 we have God's answer to Daniel's prayer
and supplication....In his desperate prayer, Daniel requested
that God recover the holy land, send His people back, and
rebuild the holy city (vv. 15-19). But God answered him by giving
him the report through the angel Gabriel of the seventy weeks
(vv. 20-27). This answer exceeded what Daniel requested.

Verses 24 through 27 are the contents of the vision. The contents are the seventy weeks....The seventy weeks are the destiny
apportioned by God for His people and for His holy city (v. 24a)....
The purpose of the seventy weeks is to close the transgression, to

make an end of sins, to make propitiation for iniquity, to bring in the righteousness of the ages, to seal up vision and prophet, and to anoint the Holy of Holies (v. 24b). Today in the old creation under human government, transgression, sins, and iniquity are prevailing. When Christ comes to crush human government, at the time appointed, the transgression will be closed, sins will be ended, and iniquity will be propitiated.

Then the righteousness of the ages will be brought in. The expression *of the ages* is a Hebrew idiom which means "eternity" or "eternal." Hence, the righteousness of the ages is an eternal righteousness. The coming kingdom age will be an age of divine righteousness, and in the new heaven and new earth, there will be eternal righteousness (2 Pet. 3:13).

Daniel 9:24b also speaks of the sealing up of vision and prophet. The vision and prophet will be sealed because everything will be fulfilled. There will, therefore, be no need of visions or prophets. In the kingdom age, there will be kings and priests but no prophets.

The last aspect of the purpose of the seventy weeks is to anoint the Holy of Holies. At the time of Daniel's prayer, the Holy of Holies was contaminated, defiled, and devastated. But when the apportioned time comes, the Holy of Holies will be properly anointed. This means that the service to God will be recovered. What a blessing!

Daniel 9:24-27 tells us of the seventy weeks. The seventy weeks are divided into three parts, with each week being seven years, not seven days, in length....First, seven weeks of forty-nine years were apportioned from the issuing of the decree to restore and rebuild Jerusalem to the completion of the rebuilding (v. 25)....Second, sixty-two weeks of four hundred thirty-four years were apportioned from the completion of the rebuilding of Jerusalem to the cutting off of the Messiah (vv. 25-26)....Finally, in verse 27 we have the one week of seven years. This week will be for Antichrist to make a firm covenant with the people of Israel. (*Life-study of Daniel,* pp. 86-88)

Further Reading: Life-study of Daniel, msg. 14; *Life-study of Jeremiah,* msg. 22

Enlightenment and inspiration: _____

_____

_____

_____

Morning Nourishment

Dan. **And after the sixty-two weeks Messiah will be cut off;...**
9:26-27 **and the people of the prince who will come will**
destroy the city and the sanctuary....And he will make
a firm covenant with the many for one week; and in the
middle of the week he will cause the sacrifice and
the oblation to cease and will replace the sacrifice and the
oblation with abominations of the desolator...

The cutting off of Messiah—the crucifixion of Christ—was the termination of the old creation with the human government in the old creation and the germination through the resurrection of Christ of God's new creation with God's eternal kingdom as the divine administration in God's new creation. Thus, the cross of Christ is the centrality and universality of God's work.

This word concerning Messiah's being cut off is not bad news but good news. Through His death on the cross, Christ terminated the old creation. Then in His resurrection He became the life-giving Spirit (1 Cor. 15:45b) to germinate those whom God has chosen and make them a new creation. (*Life-study of Daniel,* pp. 87-88)

Today's Reading

Between the sixty-ninth week and the last week, there is a gap which has already lasted for nearly two thousand years. In this gap the church is being secretly and mysteriously built by Christ in His resurrection to be the Body of Christ and bride of Christ. Also, in this gap Israel has been suffering, having lost their fathers' homeland and having been scattered. Nevertheless, God has not forgotten His people Israel but continues to grant them some degree of mercy. Eventually, the last week of seven years will come. (*Life-study of Daniel,* p. 88)

In 2 Thessalonians 2:4 Paul gives a further description of Antichrist: "Who opposes and exalts himself above all that is called God or an object of worship, so that he sits in the temple of God, setting himself forth, saying that he is God." This fulfills the prophecy concerning Antichrist in Daniel 11:36 and 37. This will take place in the midst of the last week, as prophesied in Daniel 9:27.

The temple of God mentioned in 2 Thessalonians 2:4 is "the holy place" in Matthew 24:15. [This] indicates that the temple of God will be rebuilt before the Lord comes back. The temple was destroyed more than nineteen centuries ago. But this verse says that Antichrist will seat himself in the temple of God....The nation of Israel has been formed again, and the city of Jerusalem has been returned to Israel. However, the temple has not yet been built....One day, this temple will be rebuilt, and, according to the prophecy of Daniel, Antichrist will seat himself in it. (*Life-study of 2 Thessalonians,* p. 17)

Whereas the first part of Daniel 9:26 speaks of the death of Christ, the remainder of this verse [says that]..."the people of the prince who will come will destroy the city and the sanctuary" (v. 26b). This reveals that the prince of the Roman Empire, Titus, would come with his army to destroy the city and the sanctuary—the temple....This destruction took place in A.D. 70. As Daniel 9:26c goes on to say, the end of it would be with a flood, and even to the end there would be war. The desolations have been determined.

Antichrist will make a firm covenant with the people of Israel, promising to be for them. The covenant he makes with them will be a peace agreement. However, in the middle of the seventieth week, Antichrist will change his mind, fight against God, and cause the sacrifice and oblation to cease (v. 27b). This will be the beginning of the great tribulation (Matt. 24:21), which will last for three and a half years. During the great tribulation, both the faithful Jews and the Christians still on earth will suffer Antichrist's persecution.

After he causes the sacrifice and the oblation to cease, Antichrist will replace them with the abominations (the idols of the Antichrist—2 Thes. 2:4) of the desolator (Dan. 9:27c). This desolator is Antichrist himself....Eventually, the complete destruction that has been determined will be poured out upon the desolator, Antichrist (v. 27d). (*Life-study of Daniel,* pp. 88-89)

Further Reading: The Prophecy of the Four "Sevens" in the Bible,
   ch. 1; *Life-study of 2 Thessalonians,* msgs. 2-3

Enlightenment and inspiration: _____

_____

_____

Morning Nourishment

Col. 2:2 ...Being knit together in love and unto all the riches
of the full assurance of understanding, unto the full
knowledge of the mystery of God, Christ.
Eph. By which, in reading *it*, you can perceive my under-
3:4, 6 standing in the mystery of Christ,...that in Christ
Jesus the Gentiles are fellow heirs and fellow members of the Body and fellow partakers of the promise
through the gospel.

The seventh trumpet closes the present age of mystery [Rev.
10:7]. Daniel 9:24 speaks of the seventy weeks, which were apportioned out to "seal up vision and prophet." To seal up vision and
prophet is to close the age of mystery.

To seal up vision and prophet is to finish the mystery of God. In
the church age, the age of grace, everything concerning Christ and
the church is a mystery (Eph. 5:32), but when the seventh trumpet
is sounded, the age of mystery will be over. (*The Prophecy of the
Four "Sevens" in the Bible,* pp. 49, 73)

Today's Reading

When the seventh angel is about to trumpet, the mystery of God
will be finished. In the dispensation from Adam to Moses, and from
Moses to Christ, everything was unveiled, manifested, and there
was no mystery. It will be the same in the dispensation of the
millennial kingdom and in the new heaven and the new earth—
everything will be unveiled and there will be no more mystery. But
in the dispensation from Christ to the millennial kingdom, everything is a mystery. The incarnation of Christ, as the beginning of
this dispensation of mystery, is a mystery (1 Tim. 3:16). Christ
Himself (Col. 2:2), the church (Eph. 3:4-6), the kingdom of the heavens (Matt. 13:11), the gospel (Eph. 6:19), the indwelling of Christ
(Col. 1:26-27), and the coming resurrection and transfiguration of
the saints as the ending of this dispensation of mystery (1 Cor.
15:51-52) are all mysteries which were hidden in times of the ages
(Rom. 16:25; Eph. 3:5; Col. 1:26). All these mysteries will be over,

completed, and finished at the trumpeting of the seventh trumpet. At the trumpeting of the seventh trumpet, not only God's judgment of wrath upon the earth, but also "the mystery of God is finished" [Rev. 10:7]. (*Life-study of Revelation,* pp. 311-312)

God is a mystery, and God has a mystery. What is the mystery of God? The mystery of God is Christ (Col. 2:2). All that God is and everything that He has in Himself is in Christ. All the riches, all the divine nature, and all the fullness of the Godhead dwell bodily in Christ (v. 9). Christ embodies everything that God is and everything that God has.

In this universe there is a divine mystery, and this mystery is of two parts. The first part of this mystery is the mystery of God, which is Christ Himself (1 Cor. 2:1-2). All that God is, and everything related to God, is embodied in Christ. Thus, if you do not know Christ, you do not know the mystery of God, and if you are not in Christ, you are not in the mystery of God. Further, if you do not have Christ in your spirit, you do not have any share in the mystery of God. If you want to know God and contact God, you have to be in Christ, because everything of God is embodied in Christ and Christ is the mystery of God.

The second part of the one divine mystery in this universe is the mystery of Christ. The mystery of Christ is different from the mystery of God. The mystery of Christ is the Body of Christ, the church (Eph. 3:4, 6). Thus, if you would like to meet Christ, know Christ, and receive something of Christ, you must contact the Body of Christ, the church. Just as Christ is the mystery of God, the church is the mystery of Christ. These are the two parts of the one divine mystery in this universe. (*The Mystery of God and the Mystery of Christ,* pp. 9, 81-82)

Christ and the church as one spirit (1 Cor. 6:17), typified by a husband and wife as one flesh, are the great mystery. (Eph. 5:32, footnote 1)

Further Reading: The Mysteries in God's New Testament Economy, chs. 1-3; *Basic Training,* msg. 1

Enlightenment and inspiration: _____

_____

_____

_____

Morning Nourishment

Heb. Now faith is the substantiation of things hoped for,
11:1 the conviction of things not seen.
Eph. And for me, that utterance may be given to me in
6:19 the opening of my mouth, to make known in boldness the mystery of the gospel.

The things of the Spirit are apprehended by faith. Ephesians 3:17 says, "That Christ may make His home in your hearts through faith." First Timothy 1:4 speaks of "God's economy, which is in faith." We know that Christ is making His home in our hearts through faith. Likewise, through faith we realize that God has an economy, and without faith we cannot realize God's economy. God's requirement for us related to everything in the New Testament is faith. If we do not believe, we cannot apprehend anything spiritual. We know there is a God, Christ, and the Spirit through faith. By faith we know that Christ is in the heavens and also in our spirit. By faith we know that the Bible is the Word of God, and by faith we know that we have been saved, regenerated, and forgiven by God. By faith we are sanctified, transformed, renewed, and eventually glorified. By faith we also are overcomers. Everything spiritual is apprehended by faith.

Anything that is apprehended by faith is a mystery. For this reason, the present age is the age of faith and the age of mystery. (*Messages to the Trainees in Fall 1990,* pp. 60-61)

Today's Reading

Faith assures us of the things not seen, convincing us of what we do not see. Therefore, it is the evidence, the proof, of things unseen.

Faith, which is the way to realize and enjoy the things of God, is not a part of our natural being. It is a divine ability which has been infused into us. The proper faith is the divine element, even God Himself, infused into our being as the ability to substantiate the things which we do not see. This infused element is our substantiating ability. Whenever we contact God or listen to His word, the substantiating ability which has been infused into our being by God Himself spontaneously begins to realize the things of God, the things hoped for, and the things not seen, and we simply believe. As we have seen, faith is a special sense in addition to the five senses derived from our natural birth. This sense substantiates the things of God, things which we do not see. Since the Christian life is a life of hope and in this life we aim at things unseen, we need more of the transfusion and infusion of God that we may have the ability, the faith, to substantiate the things hoped for and to have the conviction of things unseen. (*Life-study of Hebrews,* p. 535)

Second Corinthians 4:18 says, "Because we do not regard the things which are seen but the things which are not seen; for the things which are seen are temporary, but the things which are not seen are eternal." The things seen are of the temporary affliction, but the things not seen are of the eternal glory. Paul did not care for the affliction, the environment, the poverty, the opposition, the persecution, or the grinding. Those things, things which are seen, are temporary. He cared only for eternal things. (*Life-study of 2 Corinthians,* pp. 101-102)

The mystery of the gospel is Christ and the church for the fulfillment of God's eternal purpose. Some Christians preach a gospel in which there is no mystery. But Paul declared the mystery of the gospel. This mystery implies the entire New Testament economy. Christ is the mystery of God, and the church is the mystery of Christ. Both Christ and the church are for God's economy, which also is a mystery. All these mysteries are related to the gospel.

I believe that the Lord intends for a gospel preaching atmosphere to be developed in all the local churches. Pray for such an atmosphere to become prevailing.

Our burden is to make known the mystery of the gospel. Pray about this. Pray that the Lord will give us utterance and open our mouths with boldness to teach and to preach the mystery of the gospel. We all need to declare the gospel in this uplifted way. (*Life-study of Ephesians,* pp. 555-556)

Further Reading: Messages to the Trainees in Fall 1990, chs. 3, 8;
    Life-study of Ephesians, msg. 66

Enlightenment and inspiration: _____

_____

_____

_____

Morning Nourishment

2 Pet. **And we have the prophetic word** *made* **more firm,**
1:19 **to which you do well to give heed as to a lamp shin-**
     ing in a dark place, until the day dawns and the
     morning star rises in your hearts.
Matt. **Watch therefore, for you do not know on what day**
24:42 **your Lord comes.**

What Daniel received regarding the seventy weeks was not
only a vision but also a report. Daniel understood the seventy
weeks, but because we are near the end of the gap, I believe that
we understand this matter even better than Daniel did. By
studying the vision of seventy weeks in relation to God's economy, we will be helped to know where we are, what we should be,
and what we should be doing today. (*Life-study of Daniel*, p. 89)

Today's Reading

We want to go on to see the shining of the prophetic word in the
Scriptures made more firm [2 Pet. 1:19]....The Old Testament
prophecies were made firm by Jesus Christ the Lord and by some
of the apostles in the prophecies of the New Testament....What
we have today is the prophecies made more firm to us. In the New
Testament age, the shining of the prophetic word is stronger and
the warning is also stronger. (*The Prophecy of the Four "Sevens" in
the Bible*, pp. 84-85)

Having realized that the Lord will come again, we need to have
a proper attitude toward His coming. Hearing a message on His
coming and knowing the doctrine of His coming are not the end; we
have to be those who wait for His coming. We have to read the pas-
sages concerning the Lord's coming to new ones right after they believe. This will make them *persons* who "await His Son from the
heavens" [1 Thes. 1:10]....We do not search with curiosity the
prophecies concerning His second coming. [Instead,] a Christian
who lives on earth today should adopt a waiting attitude for the
Lord's return. It is wrong to give up this waiting attitude. Waiting
for the Lord's return means that a man still goes about his busi-
ness, but his eyes are set on the Lord's coming. He knows that

when the Lord comes back, He will demand certain things and ask him certain questions. He waits for the Lord like a slave waiting for his master to return. While he waits, he cannot beat his fellow slaves. Rather, he has to serve faithfully and wait patiently.

A believer has been brought into the heavenly new creation. All his actions and possessions should work towards his heavenly deposit....While he is on earth, he waits for the Lord to return from heaven. He is a heavenly citizen, one who follows the teaching of the anointing. (*The Collected Works of Watchman Nee,* vol. 60, pp. 440-441)

Peter likens the word of prophecy in the Scripture to a lamp shining in a dark place (2 Pet. 1:19)....This age is a dark place in the dark night (Rom. 13:12), and all the people of the world are moving and acting in darkness. The shining of the prophetic word is in the dark age of today....The prophetic word of the Scripture, as the shining lamp to the believers, conveys spiritual light to shine in their darkness (not merely knowledge in letters for mental apprehension), guiding them to enter into a bright day, even to pass through the dark night until the day of the Lord's appearing dawns and the morning star rises in their hearts.

Because of the prophetic word, the Lord warns us to watch [Matt. 24:42]....In Luke 21:34 the Lord warns us to take heed to ourselves that our hearts may not be weighed down with debauchery and drunkenness and anxieties of life, and that day come upon us suddenly as a snare....We also need to be watchful, at every time beseeching, that we may prevail to escape all the things which are about to take place and to stand before Christ (Luke 21:36). To escape all the things which are about to take place is to be raptured to the heavens before the great tribulation to meet Christ at the beginning of His *parousia*. (*The Prophecy of the Four "Sevens" in the Bible,* pp. 92-93)

Further Reading: The Prophecy of the Four "Sevens" in the Bible,
    ch. 6; *The Up-to-date Presentation of the God-ordained Way*
    and the Signs concerning the Coming of the Christ, chs. 6-7

Enlightenment and inspiration: _____

_____

_____

_____

Morning Nourishment

Rev. **Because you have kept the word of My endurance,**
3:10 **I also will keep you out of the hour of trial...**
2 Tim. **Henceforth there is laid up for me the crown of**
4:8 **righteousness, with which the Lord, the righteous**
Judge, will recompense me in that day, and not only
me but also all those who have loved His appearing.

We...need to keep the word of Christ's endurance (Rev. 3:10). Every word that the Lord has spoken in the Bible is a word of endurance (cf. Rom. 15:4). If we keep what the Lord says, we will suffer. The Lord today is still suffering rejection and persecution with His endurance. We are the joint partakers, not only of His kingdom, but also of His endurance (Rev. 1:9). Hence, His word to us today is the word of endurance. To keep the word of His endurance, we must suffer His rejection and persecution.

We also need to overcome and keep the Lord's works until the end (Rev. 2:26)....These works include all His doings to accomplish a full redemption for us. He died and resurrected to redeem us. He is still doing something today to sanctify us, transform us, and conform us to His image. These are the Lord's works which we have to keep. (*The Prophecy of the Four "Sevens" in the Bible,* pp. 93-94)

Today's Reading

In 2 Timothy 4:10 Paul says, "Demas has abandoned me, having loved the present age." Loving the present age, the world now before our eyes, is in contrast to loving the Lord's appearing, mentioned in verse 8....The present age is the world which surrounds us, attracts us, and tempts us....Because of the attraction of the present age, Demas abandoned the apostle....If we love the Lord's appearing, we will side with Him and fight with Him for His interests. But if we love the present age, we will side with the world. We must tell the Lord, "Lord Jesus, I love You and I love Your appearing. Because I love You, I love Your appearing." (*The Conclusion of the New Testament,* p. 3687)

In the Bible, the appearing of the Lord Jesus is typified by the morning star and the sun. His appearing as the sun is to the world, and His appearing as the morning star is to the saints. The morning star appears just before dawn. Only those who are watchful at night can see it. The sun appears during the daytime, and everyone in the world can see it. First there is the appearance of the morning star, and then the sun comes out. Before our Lord Jesus appears to the people in the world, He will first appear to those who love His appearing. What a blessed hope this is!...Are you prepared to meet Him? (*The Collected Works of Watchman Nee*, vol. 34, p. 174)

According to Paul's charge in 1 Timothy 4:1, Timothy was to live in the light of the appearing of the Lord and His kingdom. Whatever the kingdom will reject in the future must be rejected in our living today. If we live in His appearing, we would certainly refrain from quarreling; we would not want to be found arguing when the Lord appears. Not many Christians regard the Lord's coming as a warning....The apostles lived with the appearing of the Lord in view. The Lord's appearing was constantly a warning to them and regulated their living. They did not dare to do certain things because they believed that the Lord could appear at any time. If we take seriously the matters of the Lord's appearing and the kingdom, they will greatly affect our daily living. The appearing of Christ must be a basic factor in our daily living. We must live today in the light of the Lord's appearing.

[In 2 Timothy 4:8] it is not a matter of a crown of grace but of a crown of righteousness. The crown of righteousness is the crown to be a king. This means when the Lord comes back, Paul will be rewarded with the manifestation of the kingdom of the heavens.

Paul says that such an award will be given to all who love the Lord's appearing. The Lord's appearing, His coming back, is a warning, an encouragement, and an incentive to us. We should love it and look forward to it with earnest expectation and joy. (*The Conclusion of the New Testament*, pp. 3685-3686)

Further Reading: The Conclusion of the New Testament, msg. 365; The Vision of the Divine Dispensing and Guidelines for the Practice of the New Way, chs. 3-4

Enlightenment and inspiration: _____

_____

_____

_____

Hymns, #956

1   Soon our Lord will come, the day is drawing nigh,
   Sound of His approaching we can hear.
Watchful we must be and always on alert
   That the Lord our hearts with rapture cheer.

   Glory! glory! Christ will come again!
   Glory! glory! We with Him shall reign!
   With a glorious body, ever with the Lord,
   Singing all His praise with glad accord.

2   Soon our Lord will come, the Morning Star appear;
   Night is deep, and soon will dawn the day.
Never with the current of the age we go,
   That from trials we'll be kept away.

3   Soon our Lord will come His servants to reward;
   Those who love Him then the crown will share.
Watchful we must be and treasure not the world,
   Love and serve the Lord, His burden bear.

4   Soon our Lord will come and in His kingdom reign;
   Satan will be bound, the world subdued.
We must fight the battle, overcome the foe,
   On His throne He then will us include.

Composition for prophecy with main point and sub-points: _____

_____
_____
_____
_____
_____
_____
_____
_____
_____
_____
_____
_____
_____
_____
_____
_____
_____
_____
_____
_____
_____
_____
_____
_____
_____
_____
_____
_____
_____
_____
_____
_____
_____
_____
_____
_____

**The Vision of God
and His Universal Dominion
and of the Coming of the Son of Man
to Receive a Kingdom
and the Necessity of Spiritual Warfare
to Bring In the Kingdom of God**

Scripture Reading: Dan. 7:1-27; 10:10—11:1; Rev. 12:10a; 11:15

Day 1   **I. According to the record in Daniel 7, Daniel saw a vision of God and His universal dominion and of the coming of the Son of Man to receive a kingdom:**
   A. "I watched / Until thrones were set, / And the Ancient of Days sat down. / His clothing was like white snow, / And the hair of His head was like pure wool; / His throne was flames of fire, / Its wheels, burning fire. / A stream of fire issued forth / And came out from before Him. / Thousands of thousands ministered to Him, / And ten thousands of ten thousands stood before Him. / The court of judgment sat, / And the books were opened" (vv. 9-10):
      1. This is a vision of God and His universal dominion, with the fire signifying that God is absolutely righteous and altogether holy (Heb. 12:29).
      2. A special court, with God's throne as the center, has been set up in the universe to judge the four human empires (Dan. 7:2-10, 26).
      3. While the struggles are taking place between the human governments, God is behind the scene, managing the world situation (Rev. 4:1-3, 10-11).
   B. "There with the clouds of heaven / One like a Son of Man was coming; / And He came to the Ancient of Days, / And they brought Him near before Him. / And to Him was given dominion, glory, and a kingdom, / That all the peoples,

nations, and languages might serve Him. / His dominion is an eternal dominion, which will not pass away; / And His kingdom is one that will not be destroyed" (Dan. 7:13-14):

1. Concerning His judgment, God has given all power and authority to Jesus Christ as the Son of Man (John 5:22, 27); hence, Daniel 7:13 and 14 describe the coming of Christ as the Son of Man.

2. The coming here is Christ's ascension after He accomplished the work of redemption (Acts 1:9; cf. Rev. 5:6-7):

   a. According to Daniel's vision, Christ accomplished redemption and immediately came to God in ascension to receive the kingdom.

   b. This is according to God's view, in which there is no time element (Dan. 7:13-14).

   c. Daniel did not see the mystery of the church, which was hidden from the ages and from the generations but has been revealed to the New Testament apostles and prophets (Eph. 3:3-11).

Day 2   3. In His ascension Christ as the Son of Man is before the throne of God to receive dominion and a kingdom (Dan. 7:13-14):

   a. After Christ as the Son of Man receives the kingdom from God, He will come back to rule over the entire world (Luke 19:12, 15).

   b. Christ's coming will terminate the entire human government on earth, and it will bring in the eternal kingdom of God (Dan. 2:34-35, 44; Rev. 12:10a; 11:15).

II. **Because a war is taking place in the spiritual world behind the physical world, there is the necessity of spiritual warfare, of fighting, to bring in the kingdom of God (Dan. 10:10—11:1; Eph. 6:10-18; Rev. 12:10a; 11:15):**

   A. "Your words were heard; and I have come because of your words. But the prince of the kingdom of

Persia withstood me for twenty-one days; but now
Michael, one of the chief princes, came to help me"
(Dan. 10:12b-13a):

1. For us to know God's economy, we need to
   see the spiritual things behind the physical
   things, the spiritual world behind the physical world (vv. 20-21).

2. It is crucial for us to see that behind the physical scene a spiritual struggle, a struggle not
   seen with human eyes, is taking place
   (vv. 12-13, 20-21):

   a. Behind the physical scene, a spiritual
      struggle, an invisible spiritual war, is
      taking place (Eph. 6:10-20).

   b. The spiritual scene in Daniel 10 includes both
      good and evil spirits that are engaged in an
      invisible spiritual war (vv. 12-13, 20-21).

   c. While Daniel was praying for twenty-one
      days, a spiritual struggle was taking place
      in the air between two spirits, one belong-
      ing to Satan and the other belonging to
      God (9:3; 10:2-3, 12):

      (1) The angelic messenger had been fight-
          ing against the prince of the kingdom
          of Persia, probably an evil spirit, a re-
          bellious angel, who followed Satan in
          his rebellion against God (v. 20a; Rev.
          12:4a).

      (2) Michael, a prince fighting for Israel,
          fought together with the angelic mes-
          senger against the evil spirits (Dan.
          10:13, 21).

   d. Isaiah 14:12-14 unveils Satan's kingdom
      of darkness and his oneness with the rulers
      of the nations.

   e. The vision in Revelation 12 unveils the true
      situation in the universe—the warfare be-
      tween God and His enemy.

   f. In our spiritual fighting, we deal not with

Day 3

things that appear on the surface but
with the power of darkness behind these
things (Eph. 2:6; 6:12).

B. The church must engage in spiritual warfare,
fighting to bring in the kingdom of God (Matt.
12:28; Eph. 6:10-18; Rev. 12:10a; 11:15):

1. "Your kingdom come; Your will be done, as
in heaven, so also on earth" (Matt. 6:10):

a. The coming of the kingdom is not automatic; if there is no prayer, the kingdom
cannot come.

Day 4

b. Genuine prayer is a joint labor with God
to bring His kingdom to the earth and to
carry out His will on earth; hence, prayer
is a spiritual battle (2 Cor. 10:4; Eph. 6:12).

2. "Now has come the salvation and the power
and the kingdom of our God and the authority of His Christ" (Rev. 12:10):

a. Along with our praying for the coming of
the kingdom of God, we need to fight for
it (Matt. 6:10; Eph. 6:10-18):

(1) In order for the kingdom of the heavens to be established, there is the need
of spiritual fighting (Matt. 12:22-29).

Day 5

(2) The responsibility of the church is to
continue the warfare that Christ fought
on earth; the church must continue
the victorious work that Christ has
carried out against Satan (Heb. 2:14;
1 John 3:8b; Col. 2:15; Psa. 149:5-9).

b. The overcoming believers fight against
Satan to usher in God's kingdom (Rev.
12:10-11).

Day 6

3. "The kingdom of the world has become the
kingdom of our Lord and of His Christ, and
He will reign forever and ever" (11:15):

a. Spiritual warfare is the warfare between
the kingdom of God and the kingdom of
Satan (Matt. 12:26, 28).

b. The purpose of spiritual warfare is to bring in the kingdom of God (Rev. 12:10).

c. The kingdom of God is the exercise of the divine will and the overthrowing of the power of Satan by the power of God (Matt. 6:10).

d. Wherever the devil has been cast out and wherever the work of the enemy has been displaced by God's power, the kingdom of God is there (12:28; Rev. 12:7-10).

4. "The kingdom and dominion and the greatness of the kingdoms under the whole heaven will be given to the people of the saints of the Most High; His kingdom is an eternal kingdom, and all the dominions will serve and obey Him" (Dan. 7:27, cf. v. 18).

Morning Nourishment

Dan. **I watched until thrones were set, and the Ancient of**
7:9-10 **Days sat down....His throne was flames of fire, its**
wheels, burning fire. A stream of fire issued forth and
came out from before Him. Thousands of thousands
ministered to Him, and ten thousands of ten thou-
sands stood before Him. The court of judgment sat,
and the books were opened.

We [need to consider] the vision in Daniel 7 concerning the
four beasts out of the Mediterranean Sea....These four beasts are
dreadful and terrible, doing whatever they desire as if there were
no God in the universe. However, this chapter reveals that the
Ancient of Days is still on the throne.

Verses 9 and 10 speak of God and His universal dominion....
"His clothing was like white snow, / And the hair of His head was
like pure wool" [v. 9a]. This signifies that God is ancient....Every-
thing around Him is fire, meaning that God is absolutely righteous
and altogether holy. Without holiness no one can see the Lord or contact Him (Heb. 12:14)....Thousands of thousands ministered to Him,
and ten thousands of ten thousands stood before Him (Dan. 7:10b).
This vast number of angels ministered to Him for His service and
stood before Him for His glory. (*Life-study of Daniel*, pp. 59-60)

Today's Reading

A special court, with God's throne as the center, has been set
up in the universe to judge the four human empires [signified by
the four wild beasts (Dan.7:10c, 26)]. Everything that is judged by
this court will be cast into the burning fire.

Darius the Mede was the first one to conquer the Babylonian
Empire. However, according to Daniel 8 a ram, signifying Persia,
was seen with two horns. The second horn was higher than the
first, referring to Cyrus the Persian who assumed power two years
later in 536 B.C. In the first year of his reign, Cyrus issued a decree
to release all the captives of Israel back to the land of their fore-
fathers and to rebuild the temple. Because Cyrus supported them,

supplied them, and protected them, Isaiah said that Cyrus was a shepherd of God to take care of God's people (44:28). Apparently, all of these struggles are merely the activities of human governments represented by the great human image in Daniel 2. Actually, God was behind the physical world managing the entire situation.

Concerning His judgment, God has given all power and authority to Jesus Christ as the Son of Man (John 5:22). Hence, Daniel 7:13 and 14 describe the coming of the Son of Man— Christ....According to verse 13a, Christ came like a Son of Man with the clouds of heaven....The Son of Man, Christ, came to the Ancient of Days and was brought near before Him (v. 13b). The coming here is Christ's ascending.

Daniel 9:26, referring to the death of Christ on the cross for our redemption, speaks of Messiah's being cut off. This was a great achievement, the work of redemption, accomplished by Christ in His first appearance on earth. After Christ accomplished the work of redemption, He ascended to the heavens. This could be mentioned in Daniel 7 because there is no time element with God. In the sight of God, immediately after accomplishing redemption, Christ ascended to the heavens, coming to God to receive the kingdom. This indicates that from God's point of view the kingdom comes right after redemption.

Like Abraham, David, and the other prophets, [Daniel] did not see the mystery of the church which has been hidden from the ages and from the generations. He did not realize that between the first and second appearing of Christ there would be a period of time during which God would do a marvelous and mysterious work based on Christ's redemption. This work is to regenerate His redeemed people and then sanctify them, renew them, transform them, and conform them to the glorious image of Christ. According to Daniel's vision, Christ accomplished redemption and then immediately came to God in ascension to receive the kingdom. (*Life-study of Daniel*, pp. 60, 92, 60-61)

Further Reading: Life-study of Daniel, msgs. 9-10

Enlightenment and inspiration: _____

_____

_____
_____

Morning Nourishment

Dan.   I watched in the night visions, and there with the
7:13-14   clouds of heaven One like a Son of Man was coming;
and He came to the Ancient of Days, and they brought
Him near before Him. And to Him was given dominion,
glory, and a kingdom, that all the peoples, nations,
and languages might serve Him. His dominion is an
eternal dominion, which will not pass away; and His
kingdom is one that will not be destroyed.

In Revelation 4 we see the scene in heaven after Christ's ascension. The throne of God is the center of the scene in chapter 4, and God is sitting on the throne ready to execute His universal administration for the fulfillment of His eternal purpose. In chapter 5 we have the same scene after Christ ascended there....The center of this scene is the worthy Lion-Lamb. (*Life-study of Revelation*, p. 223)

To Him was given...a kingdom, that all the peoples, nations, and languages might serve Him. His dominion is an eternal dominion, which will not pass away, and His kingdom is one that will not be destroyed (Dan. 7:14; Luke 19:12, 15a). This is Christ's kingdom; it is also God's kingdom. (*Life-study of Daniel*, p. 61)

Today's Reading

After [Christ] receives the kingdom from God, He will come back to rule over the entire world (Luke 19:12, 15). Christ's coming will terminate the entire human government on earth from its end to its beginning, and it will bring in the eternal kingdom of God (Dan. 2:34-35, 44). (Dan. 7:14, footnote 1)

After the visions seen by Daniel in chapters 7 through 9, Daniel saw the vision concerning the destiny of Israel. However, before we are told of the vision Daniel saw concerning Israel's destiny in chapter 11, chapter 10 shows us the spiritual world behind the physical. For us to know God's economy and to know that in God's economy Christ is the centrality and universality of God's move, we need to see the spiritual things behind the physical.... In the spiritual world Christ is the preeminent One. Therefore, in chapter 10 He is mentioned first (vv. 4-9). He is described as wearing a linen robe, being girded with a golden girdle, and having a body like beryl (vv. 5-6).

After this vision of Christ, an angelic messenger came to tell Daniel about the things behind the physical world. He told Daniel that he himself was fighting against the prince of the kingdom of Persia, a rebellious evil spirit. Then Daniel was told that there was another evil spirit, the prince of Greece (Javan). There was also the archangel Michael, who was a prince fighting for Israel.

In chapter 5 we saw how Belshazzar was indulging in debauchery and how in the same night Darius the Mede came to defeat him and kill him. We did not see that there was a spirit fighting for Darius. Daniel 11:1 says, "I, in the first year of Darius the Mede, stood up to support and strengthen him." Darius was strong even as an old man because this heavenly messenger stood up to support him and strengthen him. The angelic messenger strengthened Darius to defeat the Babylonians because the Babylonian Empire's commission from God had been completed. With the death of Belshazzar, the Babylonian Empire became the empire of Medo-Persia to carry out another commission for God. (*Life-study of Daniel*, pp. 91-92)

Satan, who, as the Daystar, son of the dawn, was one of the earliest angels (the sons of God — Job 38:7, cf. Job 1:6) created by God at the "dawn" of the universe. He was appointed by God to be the head of all the angels (Ezek. 28:14; Jude 9) and later became Satan, the adversary of God, after he rebelled against God....Because of his rebellion, Lucifer as Satan was judged by God (Isa. 14:12-15; Ezek. 28:16-19; Luke 10:18).

Isaiah 14:12-15 identifies Lucifer with Nebuchadnezzar, the king of Babylon (v. 4), thus regarding Nebuchadnezzar as a figure of Satan, as one who was one with Satan (cf. Ezek. 28:12). This unveils Satan's kingdom of darkness behind the nations (Eph. 6:12b; cf. Dan. 10:13, 20) and his oneness with the rulers of the nations. (Isa. 14:12, footnote 1)

Further Reading: Life-study of Daniel, msgs. 15-16

Enlightenment and inspiration: _____

_____

_____

_____

Morning Nourishment

Eph. Put on the whole armor of God that you may be
6:11 able to stand against the stratagems of the devil.
Rev. ...Now has come the salvation and the power and the
12:10 kingdom of our God and the authority of His Christ,
for the accuser of our brothers has been cast down,
who accuses them before our God day and night.

I am burdened that we would all see the vision in Revelation chapter 12. Do not think that the portrait here is a small picture showing a few insignificant matters. No, it is a great vision regarding what is taking place in the entire universe. The woman in this vision has been representing the people of God since the fall of man in Genesis 3. The woman not only represents God's people, but also God Himself. In front of the woman is a dragon signifying God's enemy. Throughout the centuries, the war has been between the woman and the serpent, the dragon. (*Life-study of Revelation,* p. 447)

Today's Reading

This vision unveils the true situation in the universe. The worldly people can see only the obvious outward things: commerce, politics, industry, education, war....They only know to obtain an education that they may have a good job to earn a good living. They do not have the vision of what is taking place in the universe. But we see clearly what is going on. A woman symbolizes God's people and represents God. In a positive sense, the wife always represents her husband....It is wonderful to have a wife to represent you in a good way. This signifies that we, the people of God, are His wife and that we need to represent Him adequately. God is the unique husband, and we, the unique wife, represent Him. But God has an enemy. Firstly, this enemy was a little serpent. Eventually, however, it became a great dragon who is now in front of us. If you do not have this vision, you will be blind, not knowing what is taking place on earth or in the universe. Praise the Lord that it is not simply a matter of education, industry, commerce, diplomacy, etc., but a matter of warfare between the people of God and God's enemy. This war has been raging throughout the centuries and it is still raging today. (*Life-study of Revelation*, pp. 447-448)

We know that which hinders the gospel is not the outward environment, but Satan. We know that which usurps men and causes them not to love the Lord is neither human ties, nor the world, nor the flesh, but the satanic power of darkness. We know also that the reason for all the confusion, striving, indifference, and corruption in the church is naught else but Satan. Therefore, we do not deal with things that appear on the surface, but, through the position and authority of ascension, we deal with the power of darkness which schemes behind these things and reigns on the earth. (*The Experience of Life*, pp. 373-374)

The work of the church on earth is to bring in the kingdom of God. All the work of the church is governed by the principle of the kingdom of God. The saving of souls is under this principle, and so is the casting out of demons and all other works as well. Everything should be under the principle of God's kingdom....We must stand on the position of the kingdom of God whenever we work, and we must apply the kingdom of God to deal with the power of Satan.

The Lord wants us to pray, "Our Father who is in the heavens, Your name be sanctified; Your kingdom come; Your will be done, as in heaven, so also on earth" (Matt. 6:9-10). If the coming of the kingdom of God was automatic, the Lord would never have taught us to pray in this way. But since the Lord asked us to pray in this way, He simply showed us that this is the work of the church. Yes, the church should preach the gospel, but much more, the church should pray to bring in the kingdom of God. Some people think that whether or not we pray, the kingdom of God will come automatically. But if we know God, we will never say this. The principle of God's work is to wait for His people to move. Then He will move. (Watchman Nee, *The Glorious Church*, p. 63)

Further Reading: Life-study of Revelation, msg. 38; The Collected Works of Witness Lee, 1963, vol. 3, pp. 331-341

Enlightenment and inspiration: _____

_____
_____
_____

Morning Nourishment

Eph. For our wrestling is not against blood and flesh but
6:12 against the rulers, against the authorities, against
the world-rulers of this darkness, against the spiritual *forces* of evil in the heavenlies.

Matt. ...If I, by the Spirit of God, cast out the demons, then the
12:28-29 kingdom of God has come upon you. Or how can anyone enter into the house of the strong man and plunder
his goods unless he first binds the strong man?...

Genuine prayer is a joint labor with God to bring His kingdom
to the earth and to carry out His will on earth. Hence, prayer is
nothing less than a spiritual battle (2 Cor. 10:2, 4; Matt. 6:10; Eph.
6:12). Prayer overturns the power of darkness and opens the way
for God's will to be executed on earth. (*The Collected Works of
Watchman Nee,* vol. 44, p. 781)

Today's Reading

Daniel and three of his friends were competent in prayer. Their
prayers brought in the kingdom....In Babylon Daniel was praying
precisely for this matter so that God's kingdom might be brought
back once more to the earth (Dan. 6:10). It was completely due to
Daniel's prayer that God was able to build the temple, restore Jerusalem, and have the dominion. Therefore, we must be clear that
whether or not God's kingdom can come and whether or not He can
rule on earth all depend on whether or not God's people will pray.
The ultimate purpose of prayer is for bringing in God's kingdom.

Along with our praying for the kingdom's coming, we need to
fight for it. The coming of the kingdom has two aspects: the reality
of the kingdom (Matt. 5:3), which is in the proper church life today
(Rom. 14:17), and the manifestation of the kingdom in the millennium, which will be brought in through the overcoming believers.
The phrase *now has come...the kingdom of our God* [in Revelation 12:10] denotes the manifestation of the kingdom of God. If we
are the overcomers, we are living in the reality of the kingdom
today....Being in the manifestation of the kingdom requires us to
be in the reality of the kingdom.

In Revelation 1:9 John tells us that he was our brother and fellow partaker in the tribulation and kingdom and endurance in Jesus. He is our companion in the kingdom. The Lord's intention in Revelation is to open up the matter of the kingdom to all the saints. Yet in the first few chapters of Revelation, the lampstands as the churches are revealed, not the kingdom. This means that, practically speaking, the churches are the kingdom. The proper church life is the reality of the kingdom....In Revelation John does not say that he is one of the members of the Body of Christ but that he is our companion in the tribulation and kingdom and endurance in Jesus. Tribulation is needed for the kingdom, and endurance is needed for tribulation. If we would enter into the kingdom, we must suffer. To bear the suffering we need a certain amount of endurance. This is not our endurance but the endurance of Jesus.... God's intention for the church is to have the kingdom, and for this, all His believers must be matured to the extent that they can live in the reality of the kingdom and bring in the manifestation of the kingdom. (*The Conclusion of the New Testament*, pp. 4298-4299)

Now we must see that in order for the kingdom of the heavens to be established, there is the need of a spiritual battle, of spiritual fighting. This fighting is implied in Matthew 12:22-37. In the establishment of the kingdom a fight is raging on. Although we have covered many things, we have not yet seen that the establishment of the kingdom requires spiritual fighting. As Christ, the heavenly King, was establishing the heavenly kingdom among men on earth, He was fighting. People, however, did not see this warfare. They saw what He did outwardly, but they did not realize what was taking place inwardly. Thus, Matthew selected another historical fact [v. 22] to point out the fighting that was going on as the King was establishing the heavenly kingdom. (*Life-study of Matthew*, pp. 407-408)

Further Reading: The Conclusion of the New Testament, msg. 421; *Life-study of Matthew*, msg. 33

Enlightenment and inspiration: _____

_____

_____

_____

Morning Nourishment

Psa. Let the faithful ones exult in glory; let them give a ring-
149:5-6 ing shout upon their beds. Let the high praises of God be
in their throats, and a two-edged sword in their hand.
9 To execute upon them the judgment written. This
honor is for all His faithful ones. Hallelujah!

In the eyes of God the church occupies a very important
place. Its position is that of being joined to Christ, and its responsibility is to continue the warfare that Christ fought on earth.
Christ the Head has ascended, but His Body is still on earth. The
church, as the Body of Christ, is His propagation, continuing His
stand and work to fight against God's enemy. (*The Collected
Works of Watchman Nee,* vol. 44, p. 777)

Today's Reading

Ephesians 1:20-23 shows us that the power which operated in
Christ not only raised Him from the dead, but caused Him to
ascend to the heavens....Through His resurrection the church
received its life, and through His ascension the church assumed
its position of authority and inherited the kingdom. In this way,
He brought heaven to earth, and His will can be done on earth, as
in the heavens. Christ ascended to the heavens and received the
heavenly authority; now He is able to bring heaven to earth. Resurrection alone is not enough; there must also be ascension.
When we stand in the heavenly position, we transcend all things.
When the Lord ascended to the heavens, He transcended all the
powers of the enemy, and God subjected all things under His feet.
(Of course, this is not fully manifested at the present time.)

Christ ascended and became "Head over all things to the
church" (Eph. 1:22). Verse 23 clearly shows that the church and
Christ are inseparable. The church is...the fullness of Christ, the
overflow of Christ. God's desire is to gain a corporate man. The
church, which is formed of individual saints who are put into
Christ, is the corporate Christ; it is the combination of all the small
portions of Christ in the saints. As the Body of Christ, the church is
the continuation of Christ. Everything that belongs to Christ

belongs to the church. The position that Christ attained is the position that the church has attained. The works that Christ accomplished are sustained and perpetuated through the church.

The cross of Christ produced the church, and the church brings in the kingdom. Hence, the church stands between the cross and the kingdom. The present age is the time for the church to practically realize the victory of Christ. The Head has overcome; now the Body must also overcome. The Lord destroyed the devil on the cross and produced the church with resurrection life. Today God is establishing His kingdom on earth through His church. The church must continue the victorious work that Christ has carried out against Satan. It is responsible for bringing heaven's will down to earth and for carrying it out on earth.

In John 12—16 Satan is spoken of as the ruler of this world... (12:31; 14:30; 16:11). Presently, he is the ruler of this world, and the nations of this world are his domain. In the millennium, he will be bound and cast into the abyss. Before that time, the church is on the earth to curb the activities of Satan. The prayer of the church is the most effective means of curbing Satan. The church is a miniature of the kingdom. Any place that manifests God's authority is a place where the kingdom is realized (Matt. 12:28). It is our responsibility to put a halt to Satan's will. Wherever the church is, Satan's authority will retreat. The church is on the earth to perpetuate and manifest Christ's victorious stand over Satan. (*The Collected Works of Watchman Nee,* vol. 44, pp. 777-778)

When there is a group of people in the church who are willing to allow Christ's authority to flow among them, this will bring Christ's kingdom to the earth. When there is a group of overcomers in the church, these overcomers will bring the authority of heaven, the kingdom of God, to the earth....The overcoming believers fight against Satan to usher in God's kingdom. (*The Conclusion of the New Testament,* pp. 4296-4297)

Further Reading: Life-study of Daniel, msg. 13; *The Collected Works of Watchman Nee,* vol. 44, msg. 95

Enlightenment and inspiration: _____

_____

_____

_____

Morning Nourishment

Col. Who delivered us out of the authority of darkness and
1:13 transferred *us* into the kingdom of the Son of His love.

Dan. And the kingdom and dominion and the greatness
7:27 of the kingdoms under the whole heaven will be
      given to the people of the saints of the Most High;
      His kingdom is an eternal kingdom...

The period in which we are living is the time for the people of
God to fight for Him on earth. From the time the Lord Jesus
came forth to minister, till the time of His second coming, all the
works the people of God are doing for Him are instances of spiritual warfare. God's desire is to rescue, through those who belong
to Him, the people who were captured by Satan, and to recover
the earth which was usurped by Satan. This rescuing and recov-
ering is, according to what the Lord has shown us in Matthew
12, the warfare between the kingdom of God and the kingdom of
Satan. (*The Experience of Life,* p. 365)

Today's Reading

Since warfare exists between the kingdoms of God and Satan,
all the spiritual work we are doing for God, whatever form it may
take, as long as it touches the things of the spiritual realm, is in
nature a warfare. For example, preaching the gospel, according to
Acts 26:18, is "to open their eyes, to turn them from darkness to
light and from the authority of Satan to God." This shows us that
preaching the gospel is not only to open men's eyes and turn them
from darkness to light, but also to deliver them from the authority
of Satan.... [According to Colossians 1:13], to be delivered from the
authority of darkness is to be delivered from the authority of
Satan or the kingdom of Satan. And to be transferred into the
kingdom of the Son of God's love is to be transferred into the kingdom of God.

The purpose of spiritual warfare is to bring in the kingdom of
God. This is a subject of great significance in the Bible. (*The
Experience of Life,* pp. 365, 357)

Many Christians do not know the true significance of the

preaching of the gospel. The Bible says that we must repent for the kingdom (Matt. 4:17). The kingdom of God is actually the exercise of the divine will. When sinners repent for the kingdom of God, they turn from the side of Satan to the side of God, which is the kingdom of God, the will of God. After a person turns from the satanic will to the divine will, he must believe in the Lord Jesus and be baptized. Through baptism he is brought out of the authority of darkness, the satanic will, and is transferred into the kingdom of the Son of God's love (Col. 1:13). (*Life-study of Ephesians,* p. 529)

The church's work and responsibility is spiritual warfare. It is a matter of the conflict between God's authority and Satan's power....Some people think that the kingdom of God simply concerns the matter of rewards. This is too low of an estimate of the kingdom of God. The Lord Jesus once explained what the kingdom of God is. He said, "But if I, by the Spirit of God, cast out the demons, then the kingdom of God has come upon you" (Matt. 12:28). What is the kingdom of God? It is the overthrowing of the power of Satan by the power of God. When the devil is unable to stand in a certain place, the kingdom has come to that place. Wherever the devil has been cast out, wherever the work of the enemy has been displaced by God's power, His kingdom is there. (Watchman Nee, *The Glorious Church,* p. 61)

According to Daniel 7:22 and 27, the kingdom and the dominion and the greatness of the kingdoms under the whole heaven will be given to the people of the saints of the Most High.

In 4:1-3 we have Nebuchadnezzar's praise concerning God in His greatness, might, eternal kingdom, and everlasting dominion. In verses 2 and 3 he said, "It pleases me to declare the signs and wonders that God the Most High has done for me. How great are His signs, / And how mighty are His wonders! / His kingdom is an eternal kingdom, / And His dominion is from generation to generation." (*Life-study of Daniel,* pp. 57, 33)

Further Reading: The Experience of Life, ch. 18; *Life-study of Ephesians,* msg. 63

Enlightenment and inspiration: _____

_____

_____

_____

Hymns, #946

1 Lo, the glory! Lo, the splendor!
     Heaven's Kingdom manifest!
  And its glorious King, our Master,
     Is by God's appointment blest.
  Once in flesh He came so lowly,
     Hated and despised by man;
  Now He comes again in glory
     To fulfill the Kingdom plan.

2 Going to receive the Kingdom
     From His God, the Ancient of Days,
  Now He cometh with the Kingdom
     And its glorious, ruling rays.
  He's "the Stone" which breaks the nations
     Into pieces lowliest,
  Which "a mountain great" becometh
     As the Kingdom manifest.

3 Lo, the earth, all lands and kingdoms,
     By the Lord and Christ possessed;
  Earth beneath their sovereign ruling
     Will be full of peace and rest.
  No more war and no more hatred
     'Twixt the nations will there be;
  But God's knowledge shall suffuse them
     As the waters fill the sea.

4 All the Christian overcomers
     Shall with Christ in glory reign,
  And the remnant saved of Israel
     Then God's priesthood shall obtain.
  As God's people shall the nations
     'Neath their rule and teaching be,
  And a glorious restoration
     All creation then shall see.

5   Satan will be bound and banished;
    From his rule will earth be freed;
    With Christ's sovereign reign and headship
    Earth will then be blessed indeed.
    All to Christ will then be subject,
    To His pow'r and to His will;
    As the Head and Center glorious,
    He God's purpose will fulfill.

Composition for prophecy with main point and sub-points: _____

_____

_____

_____

_____

_____

_____

_____

_____

_____

_____

_____

_____

_____

_____

_____

_____

_____

_____

_____

_____

_____

_____

_____

_____

_____

_____

The Victory of the Overcomers

Scripture Reading: Dan. 1—6

Day 1

I. **"Those who have insight will shine like the shining of the heavenly expanse, and those who turn many to righteousness, like the stars, forever and ever" (Dan. 12:3; cf. chs. 1—6):**

A. Everyone in the local churches should be a shining star, a duplication of the heavenly Christ as the living Star (Num. 24:17; Rev. 22:16; cf. Matt. 2:2); the stars are those who shine in darkness and turn people from the wrong way to the right way (Rev. 1:20).

B. The overcomers as the shining stars are the messengers of the churches, those who are one with Christ as the Messenger of God and who possess the present Christ as the living and fresh message sent by God to His people (v. 20—2:1; Mal. 3:1).

C. There are two ways to become an overcoming star—first, by the Bible and, second, by the sevenfold intensified Spirit:

1. "We have the prophetic word made more firm, to which you do well to give heed as to a lamp shining in a dark place, until the day dawns and the morning star rises in your hearts" (2 Pet. 1:19):

Day 2

a. Peter likened the word of prophecy in the Scripture to a lamp shining in a dark place; this indicates that (1) this age is a dark place in the dark night (Rom. 13:12), and all the people of this world are moving and acting in darkness (cf. 1 John 5:19); and (2) the prophetic word of the Scripture, as the shining lamp to the believers, conveys spiritual light that shines in their darkness (not merely knowledge in letters for their mental apprehension), guiding them to enter into a bright day,

even to pass through the dark night until
the day of the Lord's appearing dawns.

   b. Before the dawning day of the Lord's appearing, the morning star rises in the hearts
of the believers, who are illuminated and
enlightened by giving heed to the shining
word of prophecy in the Scripture; if we give
heed to the word in the Bible, which shines
as a lamp in a dark place, we will have His
rising in our hearts to shine in the darkness
of apostasy where we are today, before His
actual appearing as the morning star (Rev.
2:28; 22:16; 2 Tim. 4:8).

 2. "These things says He who has the seven Spirits of God and the seven stars" (Rev. 3:1):

   a. The seven Spirits are one with the seven
stars, and the seven stars are one with the
seven Spirits.

   b. The seven Spirits of God enable the church
to be intensely living, and the seven stars
enable her to be intensely shining.

   c. The sevenfold intensified Spirit is living
and can never be replaced by the dead letters of knowledge (2 Cor. 3:6).

   d. The seven stars are the messengers of the
churches; they are the spiritual ones in the
churches, the ones who bear the responsibility for the testimony of Jesus; they should be
of the heavenly nature and should be in a
heavenly position like stars (Rev. 1:20).

Day 3 **II. The principle of the Lord's recovery is seen
with "Daniel and his companions" (Hananiah,
Mishael, and Azariah), who were absolutely one
with God in their victory over Satan's devices
(Dan. 2:13, 17; cf. Rev. 17:14; Matt. 22:14):**

   A. In his devilish tempting of Daniel and his companions, Nebuchadnezzar changed their names, which
indicated that they belonged to God, to names that
made them one with idols (Dan. 1:6-7):

1. The name Daniel, meaning "God is my Judge," was changed to Belteshazzar, meaning "the prince of Bel," or "the favorite of Bel" (Isa. 46:1).
2. The name Hananiah, meaning "Jah has graciously given," or "favored of Jah," was changed to Shadrach, meaning "enlightened by the sun god."
3. The name Mishael, meaning "Who is what God is?" was changed to Meshach, meaning "Who can be like the goddess Shach?"
4. The name Azariah, meaning "Jah has helped," was changed to Abed-nego, meaning "the faithful servant of the fire god Nego."

B. Daniel and his companions were victorious over the demonic diet (Dan. 1):
1. Nebuchadnezzar's devilish temptation was first to seduce the four brilliant young descendants of God's defeated elect, Daniel and his three companions, to be defiled by partaking of his unclean food, food offered to idols.
2. For Daniel and his companions to eat that food would have been to take in the defilement, to take in the idols, and thus to become one with Satan (cf. 1 Cor. 10:19-21).
3. When Daniel and his companions refused to eat Nebuchadnezzar's unclean food and chose instead to eat vegetables (Dan. 1:8-16), in principle they rejected the tree of the knowledge of good and evil (cf. Gen. 3:1-6) and took the tree of life, which caused them to be one with God (cf. 2:9, 16-17).
4. The Lord's recovery is the recovery of the eating of Jesus for the building up of the church (vv. 9, 16-17; Rev. 2:7, 17; 3:20).
5. We can eat Jesus by eating His words and by being careful to contact and be with those who call on Him out of a pure heart (Jer. 15:16; 2 Tim. 2:22; 1 Cor. 15:33; Prov. 13:20.)

Day 4 C. Daniel and his companions were victorious over the devilish blinding that prevents people from seeing

the great human image and the crushing stone as
the divine history within human history (Dan. 2):

1. The corporate Christ as the stone and the mountain, the Bridegroom with His bride, the corporate
man of God with the breath of God, will crush
and slay Antichrist and his armies by the
breath, the sword, of His mouth (vv. 34-35, 44-45;
2 Thes. 2:8; Rev. 19:11-21; Gen. 11:4-9; cf. Isa.
33:22).

2. Christ produces His bride as the new creation by growth, transformation, and maturity; thus, there is the urgent need of maturity
(Col. 2:19; 2 Cor. 3:18; Rom. 12:2; Heb. 6:1a).

3. Christ as the living and precious stone, foundation stone, cornerstone, and topstone of
God's building infuses us with Himself as the
preciousness to transform us into living and
precious stones for His building (1 Pet. 2:4-8;
Isa. 28:16; Zech. 3:9; 4:7, 9-10).

D. Daniel and his companions were victorious over the
seduction of idol worship (Dan. 3; cf. Matt. 4:9-10):

1. Whatever is not the true God in our regenerated spirit is an idol replacing God; whatever
is not in the spirit or of the spirit is an idol
(1 John 5:21).

2. The enemy of the Body is the self that replaces
God with its self-interest, self-exaltation, self-
glory, self-beauty, and self-strength; in the Body
and for the Body we deny the self and do not
preach ourselves but Christ Jesus as Lord
(Matt. 16:24; 2 Cor. 4:5).

3. Daniel's companions had a true spirit of martyrdom; they stood for the Lord as the unique God
and against idol worship at the cost of their lives,
being thrown at the command of Nebuchadnezzar into a blazing furnace (Dan. 3:19-23).

4. When Nebuchadnezzar looked into the furnace, he saw four men walking in the midst of
the fire (vv. 24-25); the fourth one was the

excellent Christ as the Son of Man, who had come to be with His three suffering, persecuted overcomers and to make the fire a pleasant place in which to walk about.

5. The three overcomers did not need to ask God to deliver them from the furnace (cf. v. 17); Christ as the Son of Man—the One who is qualified and capable of sympathizing with God's people in everything (Heb. 4:15-16)—came to be their Companion and take care of them in their suffering, by His presence making their place of suffering a pleasant situation.

Day 5   E. Daniel and his companions were victorious over the covering that hinders people from seeing the ruling of the heavens by the God of the heavens (Dan. 4):

1. As those who have been chosen by God to be His people for Christ's preeminence, we are under God's heavenly rule for the purpose of making Christ preeminent (vv. 18, 23-26, 30-32; Rom. 8:28-29; Col. 1:18b; 2 Cor. 10:13, 18; Jer. 9:23-24).

2. "He is able to abase those who walk in pride" (Dan. 4:37b).

F. Daniel and his companions were victorious over the ignorance concerning the result of the debauchery before God and the insult to His holiness (ch. 5):

1. Belshazzar's taking the vessels that were for God's worship in His holy temple at Jerusalem and using them in worshipping idols was an insult to God's holiness (v. 4); he should have learned the lesson from Nebuchadnezzar's experience (4:18-37); however, he did not learn the lesson and suffered as a result (5:18, 20, 24-31).

2. "An excellent spirit and knowledge and insight, and the interpretation of dreams, the declaring of riddles, and the resolving of problems [lit., knots] were found in this Daniel" (v. 12a).

3. "You..., Belshazzar, have not humbled your

heart, though you knew all this; but you have exalted yourself against the Lord of the heavens; and they have brought the vessels of His house before you, and you and your lords, your wives, and your concubines have drunk wine from them; and you have praised the gods of silver and of gold, of bronze, iron, wood, and stone, which do not see nor hear nor know. But the God in whose hand is your breath and to whom all your ways belong, you have not honored" (vv. 22-23, cf. v. 20).

Day 6

G. Daniel and his companions were victorious over the subtlety that prohibited the faithfulness of the overcomers in the worship of God (ch. 6):

1. The center of Daniel 6 is man's prayer for the carrying out of God's economy; man's prayers are like the rails that pave the way for God's move to go on; there is no other way to bring God's economy into fullness and into fulfillment except by prayer; this is the inner secret of this chapter.

2. Daniel prayed with his windows open toward Jerusalem; through his gracious prayer God brought Israel back to their fathers' land (v. 10; cf. 1 Kings 19:12, 18).

3. "Now when Daniel came to know that the writing had been signed, he went to his house (in his upper room he had windows open toward Jerusalem) and three times daily he knelt on his knees and prayed and gave thanks before his God, because he had always done so previously" (Dan. 6:10).

4. God will listen to our prayer when our prayer is toward Christ (typified by the Holy Land), toward the kingdom of God (typified by the holy city), and toward the house of God (typified by the holy temple) as the goal in God's eternal economy (1 Kings 8:48-49).

Morning Nourishment

Dan.   And those who have insight will shine like the shin-
12:3   ing of the heavenly expanse, and those who turn many
       to righteousness, like the stars, forever and ever.
Rev.   The mystery of the seven stars which you saw upon
1:20   My right hand and the seven golden lampstands: The
       seven stars are the messengers of the seven church-
       es, and the seven lampstands are the seven churches.

Not only is Christ Himself the star [cf. Num. 24:17], but also His followers, the shining ones in the churches. In the Acts and the Epistles the leading ones were called elders or bishops, but in the last book of the Bible they are the stars. Now it is not a matter of title or position, but a matter of shining. All the living ones of the local churches must be shining stars.

What does it mean to be a star? Daniel 12:3 gives the answer: "And those who have insight will shine like the shining of the heavenly expanse, and those who turn many to righteousness, like the stars, forever and ever." The stars are those who shine in darkness and turn people from the wrong way to the right way. Now, during the church age, is the time of night; so we need the shining of the stars. All the leading ones in the local churches should never claim their position: they should never say, "I am one of the elders; you must recognize me." If they say this, they are in darkness. We need the brothers and sisters who shine; we need the shining stars. It is by the shining in today's darkness that people receive the guidance and are turned from the wrong way to the right way. Anything that is wrong is unrighteousness; anything that is right is righteousness. Those who turn many to righteousness are the stars which shine forever and ever. (*Finding Christ by the Living Star,* pp. 24-25)

Today's Reading

In the beginning of the New Testament there was only one star in the heavens, but in the end of the New Testament there are seven stars in seven local churches. In every local church there is a star; in every local church there is something shining, leading people to the right way....Today the star is in the local churches. The Bible ends with this word: "I am the Root and the Offspring of David, the bright morning star. And the Spirit and the bride say, Come!" (Rev. 22:16-17). Today the star is with the Spirit and with the bride. Where the Spirit is, there is the star; where the bride, the church, is, there is the star.

In the Bible we not only see how we may follow the star, but even become one of the stars. There are two ways: first, by the Bible; second, by the Spirit.

Second Peter 1:19 gives us the first secret: "We have the prophetic word made more firm, to which you do well to give heed as to a lamp shining in a dark place, until the day dawns and the morning star rises in your hearts." We have the prophetic word, the Bible. But the prophetic word is not the star; the Bible is not the star. Then what must we do? This verse says that since we have the prophetic word, we must give heed to it, we must pay full attention to it, until the day dawns and the morning star rises in our hearts....This star is something as phosphorous, bringing light in the darkness....If we deal with the Word livingly and properly, it surely will turn into the living Christ. This is the turning point—the Word must be turned into Christ; the written word must be turned into the living word. We can never separate Christ from the living word. We must give heed to the prophetic word until it rises within us as Christ, as the phosphorous, as the day breaking through the darkness.

To have the Bible in your hands is one thing; to give heed to the Word until the morning star rises in your heart is another. To have the knowledge of the Bible is one thing, but to have a shining star rising in your spirit is another....What we need today is to take the Word into us, to take heed to the living word until something within rises and shines in our heart. Then we will have the star, and then we will be a star. This is not just the knowledge about Christ, but Christ Himself as the living star. (*Finding Christ by the Living Star,* pp. 25-28)

Further Reading: Finding Christ by the Living Star

Enlightenment and inspiration: _____

_____

_____

_____

Morning Nourishment

2 Pet. **And we have the prophetic word *made* more firm,**
1:19 **to which you do well to give heed as to a lamp shin-**
ing in a dark place, until the day dawns and the
morning star rises in your hearts.
Rev. **And to the messenger of the church in Sardis write:**
3:1 **These things says He who has the seven Spirits of**
God and the seven stars: I know your works, that you
have a name that you are living, and yet you are dead.

Peter likened the word of prophecy in the Scripture to a lamp
shining in a dark place. This indicates that (1) this age is a dark
place in the dark night (Rom. 13:12), and all the people of this world
are moving and acting in darkness; and (2) the prophetic word of
the Scripture, as the shining lamp to the believers, conveys spiritual light that shines in their darkness (not merely knowledge in
letters for their mental apprehension), guiding them to enter into a
bright day,...the day of the Lord's appearing....Before the Lord as
the sunlight appears, we need this word as light to shine over our
footsteps. (2 Pet. 1:19, footnote 2)

[*The day dawns* is] a metaphor illustrating a coming time that
will be full of light, as a bright day dawning, with the morning star
rising, before its dawning, in the hearts of the believers, who are
illuminated and enlightened by giving heed to the shining word of
prophecy in the Scripture....This will cause and encourage them
to earnestly seek the Lord's presence and be watchful so that they
will not miss the Lord in the secret part of His coming (parousia),
when He will come as a thief....Hence, this metaphor must allude
to the coming age, the age of the kingdom, as a day that will dawn
at the appearing (the coming) of the Lord (v. 16) as the Sun of
righteousness (Mal. 4:2), whose light will shine to break through
the gloom of the dark night of this age. (2 Pet. 1:19, footnote 4)

Today's Reading

In the darkest hour of the night the Lord will appear as the
morning star (Rev. 2:28; 22:16) to those who are watchful and
looking for His dear appearing (2 Tim. 4:8). They have been

enlightened by the shining of the prophetic word, which is able to lead them to the dawning day. If we give heed to the word in the Bible,...we will have His rising in our hearts to shine in the darkness of apostasy where we are today, before His actual appearing as the morning star. (2 Pet. 1:19, footnote 4)

The seven Spirits of God enable the church to be intensely living, and the seven stars enable her to be intensely shining. To the church in Ephesus, Christ was the One who held the seven stars and walked in the midst of the seven lampstands. The initial church needed the care of Christ, and her leaders needed His keeping grace. To the church in Smyrna, He was the One who became dead and lived again. The suffering church needed the resurrection life of Christ. To the church in Pergamos, Christ was the One who has the sharp two-edged sword. The degraded, worldly church needed His judging and slaying word. To the church in Thyatira, He was the One who has eyes like flaming fire and feet like shining bronze. The apostate church needed His searching and judging.... To the church in Sardis, He was the One who has the seven Spirits of God and the seven stars. The dead, reformed church needed the sevenfold intensified Spirit of God and the shining leaders. The sevenfold intensified Spirit is living and can never be replaced by the dead letters of knowledge (2 Cor. 3:6). (Rev. 3:1, footnote 2)

In 2 Peter we have the prophetic word, but in Revelation we have the seven Spirits. Revelation 3:1 says, "These things says He who has the seven Spirits of God and the seven stars." The hand of Jesus not only holds the seven stars but also the seven Spirits. This means that the seven Spirits are one with the seven stars, and the seven stars are one with the seven Spirits. If we have the living word as the morning star rising within us and we are one with the seven Spirits, eventually we will become the stars. We not only have the star shining within us, but by looking to the star and following in the Spirit we become the stars. (*Finding Christ by the Living Star,* pp. 30-31)

Further Reading: Finding Christ by the Living Star

Enlightenment and inspiration: _____

_____

_____

_____

Morning Nourishment

Dan. But Daniel set his heart not to defile himself with the
1:8   king's choice provision...
16   Therefore the steward withheld their *portion of* the
      choice provision and the wine that they were to
      drink and gave them vegetables.
2:17 Then Daniel went to his house and made the thing
      known to Hananiah, Mishael, and Azariah, his
      companions.

In his devilish temptation of Daniel and his companions, Nebuchadnezzar also changed their names, which indicated that they belonged to God, to names that made them one with the idols [Dan. 1:6-7]. The name of Daniel, meaning "God is the Judge," or "God is my Judge," was changed to Belteshazzar—"the prince of Bel," or "the favorite of Bel" (Isa. 46:1). The name of Hananiah, which means "Jehovah is kind," or "the favorite of Jehovah," was changed to Shadrach— "enlightened by the sun god." The name of Mishael means "Who can be like God?" but his name was changed to Meshach—"Who can be like the goddess Shach?" The name of Azariah, which means "Jehovah is my help," was changed to Abed-nego—"the faithful servant of the fire god Nego." (*Life-study of Daniel*, p. 10)

Today's Reading

In principle, all the temptations that come to us are related to eating. Nebuchadnezzar's devilish temptation was first to seduce Daniel and his three companions, the four brilliant young descendants of God's defeated elect, to be defiled in partaking of his unclean food, food offered to idols. Nebuchadnezzar provided Daniel and his three companions with the choice food to eat. To Daniel, that choice food was actually the tree of the knowledge of good and evil. That tree is something attached to Satan and even one with Satan, but the tree of life is something attached to God and one with God. To eat of the tree of the knowledge of good and evil is to become attached to Satan; to eat of the tree of life is to become attached to God. When Daniel and his companions refused to eat Nebuchadnezzar's unclean food and chose instead to eat vegetables, they were actually rejecting the tree of the knowledge of good and evil and taking the tree of life.

The choice food was defiling, not clean, for it had been offered to Nebuchadnezzar's gods. For Daniel and his companions to eat that food would have been...to take in the idols, and thus to become one with Satan. If they had done this, God would have been finished and would have had nothing on earth for Himself and His interest. Then Satan could have boasted and said, "God, You have been completely defeated. You have nothing on earth to represent You and to be one with You." God had been defeated in His elect. Now if their descendants in the captivity, the younger generation, had followed in the steps of their fathers, God would have been fully defeated. But Daniel and his companions were for God. They were attached to God, they cleaved to God, and they were one with God because they took God in.

To eat Nebuchadnezzar's choice food is to take Satan as our supply and to become one with Satan....If we are careless in our eating, in our shopping, in where we go, and in what we do, we may take in something related to idols, something demonic. We are what we eat. If we eat godly food—that is, if we eat God-food, God as our food—we will be one with God.

In Daniel 1...first, we [see] the figure of a fighting, overcoming general, Nebuchadnezzar, who has just returned from Jerusalem to Babylon with many captives following behind him. Second, we see four brilliant young men among the captives. Third, these young men are specially chosen from among the captives and then presented with the king's choice food. Fourth, they set their hearts to keep themselves for God, and they reject the royal food and eat vegetables only. Nevertheless, the four become very pleasant, happy, and healthy. Then as a result, God's presence, wisdom, and insight are with them, and they can understand things ten times better than all the others in Nebuchadnezzar's realm. (*Life-study of Daniel,* pp. 9-10, 31-32)

Further Reading: Life-study of Daniel, msg. 2

Enlightenment and inspiration: _____

_____

_____

Morning Nourishment

Dan. ...Our God whom we serve is able to deliver us from
3:17-18 the blazing furnace of fire, and He will deliver *us* out
of your hand....But if *He does* not, let it be known to
you, O king, that we will not serve your gods nor
worship the golden image that you have set up.

25 ...Look, I see four men loose, walking in the midst
of the fire; and they are not harmed. And the
appearance of the fourth is like a son of the gods.

In [Daniel 3 we see] the victory of the young descendants of
God's degraded elect over the seduction of idol worship.

Daniel's three companions, the young overcomers among the
Jewish captives, stood against the devilish worship and were
accused by the Chaldeans (vv. 8-12). The Chaldeans were jealous
of Daniel and his companions and took their refusal to worship
the golden image as grounds to accuse them before Nebuchadnezzar. (*Life-study of Daniel,* pp. 25-26)

Today's Reading

Nebuchadnezzar, in rage and fury, tempted the young overcomers by giving them another chance to worship his golden
image, with the threat of throwing them into a blazing furnace of
fire (Dan. 3:13-15).

The three overcomers answered, "If it be so, our God whom we
serve is able to deliver us from the blazing furnace of fire, and He
will deliver us out of your hand, O king" (v. 17). Their response to
Nebuchadnezzar was impolite and very bold (vv. 16-18). Yet there
was still something of the natural thought in their response. They
said that God was able to deliver them *from* the blazing furnace.
Actually, God did not need to deliver them from the furnace. He
kept them in the furnace and made the fire of no effect (v. 25).
They were bold, but they were not so spiritual. If they had been
spiritual, they would have said, "Nebuchadnezzar, we are happy
to go into the blazing furnace, because when we go He comes. He
makes your burning furnace a very pleasant place."

Nebuchadnezzar was filled with fury, and the countenance of his face was changed toward the young overcomers. He commanded that the furnace be made seven times hotter than usual, and that certain mighty men in his army bind the overcomers and throw them into the blazing furnace of fire (vv. 19-21)....The mighty men were slain by the flame of the fire, and the three young overcomers fell into the blazing furnace of fire bound up (vv. 22-23).... Nebuchadnezzar was astonished and said to his counselors, "Did we not throw three men into the midst of the fire bound up?... Look, I see four men loose, walking in the midst of the fire; and they are not harmed. And the appearance of the fourth is like a son of the gods" (vv. 24-25). This fourth one was Christ. Christ had come to be with His three suffering, persecuted overcomers and to make the fire a pleasant place in which to walk about.

Our natural thought is that we need to leave the fire of our circumstances. We may think that if we have a troublesome husband or a bothersome wife, we should pray and ask God to deliver us out of such a situation. But the Lord would say, "I do not like to deliver you from this situation in your married life. Instead, I will keep you there, and I will come and make your environment a pleasant place." When the enemy throws us into the furnace, we should realize that we do not need to ask the Lord to deliver us. He will come to be with us and take care of us in our suffering, making our place of suffering a pleasant situation. (*Life-study of Daniel,* pp. 26-27)

This fourth one was the excellent Christ as the Son of Man, who had come to be with His three suffering, persecuted overcomers and to make the fire a pleasant place in which to walk about....Christ as the Son of Man — the One who is qualified and capable of sympathizing with God's people in everything (Heb. 4:15)—came to be their Companion and take care of them in their suffering, by His presence making their place of suffering a pleasant situation. (Dan. 3:25, footnote 1)

Further Reading: Life-study of Daniel, msgs. 3-5; *The Heavenly Vision,* chs. 3-4

Enlightenment and inspiration: _____

_____

_____

_____

Morning Nourishment

Dan. Now I, Nebuchadnezzar, praise and exalt and honor
4:37 the King of the heavens, because all His works are
truth and His ways justice, and because He is able
to abase those who walk in pride.

5:22-23 And you his descendant, Belshazzar,...have brought the
vessels of His house before you,...and you have praised
the gods..., which do not see nor hear nor know. But
the God in whose hand is your breath and to whom
all your ways *belong*, you have not honored.

The book of Daniel covers three crucial matters: God's heavenly rule, the preeminence of Christ, and the destiny apportioned
by God for His people. In His economy God administrates the universe, including all the kings and kingdoms on the earth, in order
to fulfill His purpose, which is that Christ should be preeminent
in all things (Col. 1:18). For Christ to be preeminent, God needs a
chosen people to coordinate and cooperate with Him. Under the
rule of the heavens, everything is working together for the good of
God's elect for the purpose of making Christ preeminent (Rom.
8:28-29). (Dan. 4:26, footnote 1)

God gave Nebuchadnezzar twelve months to repent [from his
pride]. However, Nebuchadnezzar was void of the capacity to know
God inwardly, and nothing within him was touched. Hence, there
was no repentance and no change; rather, Nebuchadnezzar was
filled with pride (vv. 30, 37; 5:20) and thus came under God's judgment (Prov. 16:18; 1 Pet. 5:5). (Dan. 4:29, footnote 1)

Today's Reading

Daniel 5...covers the victory of the young descendants of God's
degraded elect over the ignorance concerning the result of the debauchery before God and the insult to His holiness. What Daniel
records...is based on the spiritual view for spiritual lessons.

Belshazzar (a descendant of Nebuchadnezzar and a king of
Babylon) made a great feast for a thousand of his lords, and he
drank wine before them (5:1). Here we see Belshazzar's debauchery before God. Debauchery is an overindulgence in eating and

drinking for an adulterous purpose.

Belshazzar, under the influence of the wine, commanded men to bring the gold and silver vessels that Nebuchadnezzar his forefather had taken out of the temple in Jerusalem, that he, his lords, his wives, and his concubines might drink from them and praise the gods of gold, silver, bronze, iron, wood, and stone (vv. 2-4). They took the vessels that were for God's worship in His holy temple at Jerusalem and used them in worshipping idols. That was an insult to God's holiness.

In chapter 5 concerning the case of Belshazzar, we see the importance of being serious with God and not disregarding any spiritual lesson. Belshazzar did not benefit from the lesson learned by his forefather Nebuchadnezzar in chapter 4. The case of Nebuchadnezzar teaches us that we need to be careful and not consider what we have achieved. The palace built by Nebuchadnezzar was vast. When he took a walk on the roof of that palace, he became proud and said, "Is this not Babylon the great, which I have built up as a royal house by the might of my power and for the glory of my majesty?" (4:30). This should warn us that our achievement may make us proud, and this may usher in God's judgment. God's judgment upon Nebuchadnezzar reduced him to nothing. This was the reason he could say of the Lord, "All the inhabitants of earth are considered as nothing, / But He does according to His will in the army of heaven / And among the inhabitants of the earth; / And there is no one who can resist His hand / Or say to Him, What are You doing?" (4:35). In 4:37 concerning the Lord, Nebuchadnezzar went on to say, "He is able to abase those who walk in pride." Belshazzar should have learned the lesson from Nebuchadnezzar's experience; however, he did not learn the lesson and suffered as a result.

Belshazzar's situation should make a deep impression on us. We all need to see that if we have received some lesson from God, we must regard that very seriously. If we disregard any lesson, we will suffer. (*Life-study of Daniel,* pp. 39-40, 43-44)

Further Reading: Life-study of Daniel, msgs. 6-7

__Enlightenment and inspiration:__ _____

_____

_____

_____

Morning Nourishment

Dan. **Now when Daniel came to know that the writing**
6:10-11 **had been signed, he went to his house (in his upper**
room he had windows open toward Jerusalem)
and three times daily he knelt on his knees and
prayed and gave thanks before his God, because
he had *always* **done so previously. Then these men**
assembled and found Daniel making petition and
supplication before his God.

Daniel 6 is very crucial because it shows us how God carries out His economy with His elect for Christ's coming. God desires to carry out His economy, but man is needed to pray for His economy on earth. God carries out His economy on the earth through His faithful channels of prayer. Satan's strategy is to frustrate the prayer which is for God's move. Thus, the center of this chapter is man's prayer for the carrying out of God's economy.

God's move is like a train which must have rails for its move. Man's prayers are like the rails which pave the way for God's move to go on. There is no other way to bring God's economy into fullness and into fulfillment except by prayer. This is the inner secret of this chapter. (*Life-study of Daniel,* p. 45)

Today's Reading

In Daniel 6:4 through 9 we see the subtle attack of Satan on Daniel concerning the worship of God....Being jealous of Daniel, the chief ministers and satraps "sought to find a ground for accusation against Daniel from the perspective of the kingdom, but they could find no ground for accusation or fault, inasmuch as he was faithful, and no negligence or fault was found related to him" (v. 4). Therefore,...[they] took counsel together that the king should establish a statute and make firm an edict that anyone who made a petition within the next thirty days to any god or man besides the king should be cast into the lions' den (vv. 5-7). They appealed to the king, saying, "Now, O king, establish the edict and sign the writing, so that it is not changed, according to the law of the Medes and Persians, which cannot pass away" (v. 8). The intention of the chief ministers and satraps was to destroy Daniel, but Satan, who was behind them, wanted to stop or cut off the channel of prayer God was using for the carrying out of His economy.

Daniel had read the prophecy of Jeremiah which prophesied that the children of Israel would serve the king of Babylon for seventy years (9:2b; Jer. 25:11). Standing upon this word, Daniel must have prayed many times for the fulfillment of this prophecy and for the return of the captives. He prayed, and he would not let anything stop or frustrate his prayer. He knew that his prayer was for the carrying out of God's economy concerning His elect. Therefore, his prayer was a serious matter. Today, prayer is the lifeline in the Lord's recovery. The more Satan tries to frustrate our prayer, the more we should pray.

Daniel 6:25-28 reveals God's victory over Satan in the worship of God on earth, even in a Gentile kingdom, through the overcomers in the captivity of His defeated elect....Daniel's victory over the subtlety that prohibited the faithfulness of the overcomers in the worship of God was the last step of the victory over Satan's devices. Without these overcomers, God would have been fully defeated by Satan, having nothing on earth for Himself.

When Satan sent Nebuchadnezzar to destroy the holy city with the temple in order to take away God's worship and service, it seemed that God was defeated and that His interest, worship, and service on earth were destroyed. Yet under God's sovereignty, four of the young men selected by Nebuchadnezzar to stand in the king's palace became overcomers to keep God's worship and service. God had four young overcomers living in the palace day by day, yet they were absolutely one with God. This was a shame to Satan and a boast to God....Today, as long as there are some overcomers on this earth, regardless of the number, God will have reason to boast. When God sees today's overcomers standing on the ground of the church, He will be happy and pleased. (*Life-study of Daniel*, pp. 46-50)

Further Reading: Life-study of Daniel, msg. 8

Enlightenment and inspiration: _____

_____

_____

_____

Hymns, #893

1   Conflict today is fierce,
      The strength of Satan more;
  The cry of battle calling now
      Is louder than before.
      The rebel voice of hell
      E'en stronger now becomes;
  But list, the midnight cry resounds,
      Behold, I quickly come!

2   Trials more bitter grow,
      The fighting doth enlarge;
  Hell's forces rally all their pow'rs
      And gather for the charge.
      Yet while we wait and watch
      And feel the war severe,
  We hear the joyful song ring out,
      Jesus, the Lord, is near!

3   'Tis harder at the end
      The word to testify,
  For Satan fights with all his pow'r
      Our witness to defy.
      Much greater strength we need
      The foe to overcome;
  How happy when the Lord we see
      And all our sighing's done!

4   Who then will forward go
      Strong in His mighty power?
  Who then will firmly trust the Lord
      Until the vict'ry hour;
      Till with the conqu'rors blest,
      The triumph song's begun?
  That man will then rejoice to hear,
      Behold, I quickly come!

5   Who then will choose God's best,
      And take the narrow track,
  Though passing thru the wildest storms,
      Yet never turning back?
      Who now will dare press on,
      Enduring pain and fear?
  All such will then rejoice to see
      Jesus, the Lord, is near!

6   Though deep the darkness be
We still would onward go,
Till we the day of rapture greet
And glory 'round shall glow.
'Tis there we'll see the Lord,
And Satan overcome;
The overcomers will rejoice,
Jesus, the Lord, has come!

Composition for prophecy with main point and sub-points: _____

_____

_____

_____

_____

_____

_____

_____

_____

_____

_____

_____

_____

_____

_____

_____

_____

_____

_____

_____

_____

_____

_____

_____

_____

_____

_____

Reading Schedule for the Recovery Version of the Old Testament with Footnotes

Wk.	Lord's Day	Monday	Tuesday	Wednesday	Thursday	Friday	Saturday
1	Gen. 1:1-5 ☐	1:6-23 ☐	1:24-31 ☐	2:1-9 ☐	2:10-25 ☐	3:1-13 ☐	3:14-24 ☐
2	4:1-26 ☐	5:1-32 ☐	6:1-22 ☐	7:1—8:3 ☐	8:4-22 ☐	9:1-29 ☐	10:1-32 ☐
3	11:1-32 ☐	12:1-20 ☐	13:1-18 ☐	14:1-24 ☐	15:1-21 ☐	16:1-16 ☐	17:1-27 ☐
4	18:1-33 ☐	19:1-38 ☐	20:1-18 ☐	21:1-34 ☐	22:1-24 ☐	23:1—24:27 ☐	24:28-67 ☐
5	25:1-34 ☐	26:1-35 ☐	27:1-46 ☐	28:1-22 ☐	29:1-35 ☐	30:1-43 ☐	31:1-55 ☐
6	32:1-32 ☐	33:1—34:31 ☐	35:1-29 ☐	36:1-43 ☐	37:1-36 ☐	38:1—39:23 ☐	40:1—41:13 ☐
7	41:14-57 ☐	42:1-38 ☐	43:1-34 ☐	44:1-34 ☐	45:1-28 ☐	46:1-34 ☐	47:1-31 ☐
8	48:1-22 ☐	49:1-15 ☐	49:16-33 ☐	50:1-26 ☐	Exo. 1:1-22 ☐	2:1-25 ☐	3:1-22 ☐
9	4:1-31 ☐	5:1-23 ☐	6:1-30 ☐	7:1-25 ☐	8:1-32 ☐	9:1-35 ☐	10:1-29 ☐
10	11:1-10 ☐	12:1-14 ☐	12:15-36 ☐	12:37-51 ☐	13:1-22 ☐	14:1-31 ☐	15:1-27 ☐
11	16:1-36 ☐	17:1-16 ☐	18:1-27 ☐	19:1-25 ☐	20:1-26 ☐	21:1-36 ☐	22:1-31 ☐
12	23:1-33 ☐	24:1-18 ☐	25:1-22 ☐	25:23-40 ☐	26:1-14 ☐	26:15-37 ☐	27:1-21 ☐
13	28:1-21 ☐	28:22-43 ☐	29:1-21 ☐	29:22-46 ☐	30:1-10 ☐	30:11-38 ☐	31:1-17 ☐
14	31:18—32:35 ☐	33:1-23 ☐	34:1-35 ☐	35:1-35 ☐	36:1-38 ☐	37:1-29 ☐	38:1-31 ☐
15	39:1-43 ☐	40:1-38 ☐	Lev. 1:1-17 ☐	2:1-16 ☐	3:1-17 ☐	4:1-35 ☐	5:1-19 ☐
16	6:1-30 ☐	7:1-38 ☐	8:1-36 ☐	9:1-24 ☐	10:1-20 ☐	11:1-47 ☐	12:1-8 ☐
17	13:1-28 ☐	13:29-59 ☐	14:1-18 ☐	14:19-32 ☐	14:33-57 ☐	15:1-33 ☐	16:1-17 ☐
18	16:18-34 ☐	17:1-16 ☐	18:1-30 ☐	19:1-37 ☐	20:1-27 ☐	21:1-24 ☐	22:1-33 ☐
19	23:1-22 ☐	23:23-44 ☐	24:1-23 ☐	25:1-23 ☐	25:24-55 ☐	26:1-24 ☐	26:25-46 ☐
20	27:1-34 ☐	Num. 1:1-54 ☐	2:1-34 ☐	3:1-51 ☐	4:1-49 ☐	5:1-31 ☐	6:1-27 ☐
21	7:1-41 ☐	7:42-88 ☐	7:89—8:26 ☐	9:1-23 ☐	10:1-36 ☐	11:1-35 ☐	12:1—13:33 ☐
22	14:1-45 ☐	15:1-41 ☐	16:1-50 ☐	17:1—18:7 ☐	18:8-32 ☐	19:1-22 ☐	20:1-29 ☐
23	21:1-35 ☐	22:1-41 ☐	23:1-30 ☐	24:1-25 ☐	25:1-18 ☐	26:1-65 ☐	27:1-23 ☐
24	28:1-31 ☐	29:1-40 ☐	30:1—31:24 ☐	31:25-54 ☐	32:1-42 ☐	33:1-56 ☐	34:1-29 ☐
25	35:1-34 ☐	36:1-13 ☐	Deut. 1:1-46 ☐	2:1-37 ☐	3:1-29 ☐	4:1-49 ☐	5:1-33 ☐
26	6:1—7:26 ☐	8:1-20 ☐	9:1-29 ☐	10:1-22 ☐	11:1-32 ☐	12:1-32 ☐	13:1—14:21 ☐

Reading Schedule for the Recovery Version of the Old Testament with Footnotes

Wk.	Lord's Day	Monday	Tuesday	Wednesday	Thursday	Friday	Saturday
27	14:22—15:23 ☐	16:1-22 ☐	17:1—18:8 ☐	18:9—19:21 ☐	20:1—21:17 ☐	21:18—22:30 ☐	23:1-25 ☐
28	24:1-22 ☐	25:1-19 ☐	26:1-19 ☐	27:1-26 ☐	28:1-68 ☐	29:1-29 ☐	30:1—31:29 ☐
29	31:30—32:52 ☐	33:1-29 ☐	34:1-12 ☐	Josh. 1:1-18 ☐	2:1-24 ☐	3:1-17 ☐	4:1-24 ☐
30	5:1-15 ☐	6:1-27 ☐	7:1-26 ☐	8:1-35 ☐	9:1-27 ☐	10:1-43 ☐	11:1—12:24 ☐
31	13:1-33 ☐	14:1—15:63 ☐	16:1—18:28 ☐	19:1-51 ☐	20:1—21:45 ☐	22:1-34 ☐	23:1—24:33 ☐
32	Judg. 1:1-36 ☐	2:1-23 ☐	3:1-31 ☐	4:1-24 ☐	5:1-31 ☐	6:1-40 ☐	7:1-25 ☐
33	8:1-35 ☐	9:1-57 ☐	10:1—11:40 ☐	12:1—13:25 ☐	14:1—15:20 ☐	16:1-31 ☐	17:1—18:31 ☐
34	19:1-30 ☐	20:1-48 ☐	21:1-25 ☐	Ruth 1:1-22 ☐	2:1-23 ☐	3:1-18 ☐	4:1-22 ☐
35	1 Sam. 1:1-28 ☐	2:1-36 ☐	3:1—4:22 ☐	5:1—6:21 ☐	7:1—8:22 ☐	9:1-27 ☐	10:1—11:15 ☐
36	12:1—13:23 ☐	14:1-52 ☐	15:1-35 ☐	16:1-23 ☐	17:1-58 ☐	18:1-30 ☐	19:1-24 ☐
37	20:1-42 ☐	21:1—22:23 ☐	23:1—24:22 ☐	25:1-44 ☐	26:1-25 ☐	27:1—28:25 ☐	29:1—30:31 ☐
38	31:1-13 ☐	2 Sam. 1:1-27 ☐	2:1-32 ☐	3:1-39 ☐	4:1—5:25 ☐	6:1-23 ☐	7:1-29 ☐
39	8:1—9:13 ☐	10:1—11:27 ☐	12:1-31 ☐	13:1-39 ☐	14:1-33 ☐	15:1—16:23 ☐	17:1—18:33 ☐
40	19:1-43 ☐	20:1—21:22 ☐	22:1-51 ☐	23:1-39 ☐	24:1-25 ☐	1 Kings 1:1-19 ☐	1:20-53 ☐
41	2:1-46 ☐	3:1-28 ☐	4:1-34 ☐	5:1—6:38 ☐	7:1-22 ☐	7:23-51 ☐	8:1-36 ☐
42	8:37-66 ☐	9:1-28 ☐	10:1-29 ☐	11:1-43 ☐	12:1-33 ☐	13:1-34 ☐	14:1-31 ☐
43	15:1-34 ☐	16:1—17:24 ☐	18:1-46 ☐	19:1-21 ☐	20:1-43 ☐	21:1—22:53 ☐	2 Kings 1:1-18 ☐
44	2:1—3:27 ☐	4:1-44 ☐	5:1—6:33 ☐	7:1-20 ☐	8:1-29 ☐	9:1-37 ☐	10:1-36 ☐
45	11:1—12:21 ☐	13:1—14:29 ☐	15:1-38 ☐	16:1-20 ☐	17:1-41 ☐	18:1-37 ☐	19:1-37 ☐
46	20:1—21:26 ☐	22:1-20 ☐	23:1-37 ☐	24:1—25:30 ☐	1 Chron. 1:1-54 ☐	2:1—3:24 ☐	4:1—5:26 ☐
47	6:1-81 ☐	7:1-40 ☐	8:1-40 ☐	9:1-44 ☐	10:1—11:47 ☐	12:1-40 ☐	13:1—14:17 ☐
48	15:1—16:43 ☐	17:1-27 ☐	18:1—19:19 ☐	20:1—21:30 ☐	22:1—23:32 ☐	24:1—25:31 ☐	26:1-32 ☐
49	27:1-34 ☐	28:1—29:30 ☐	2 Chron. 1:1-17 ☐	2:1—3:17 ☐	4:1—5:14 ☐	6:1-42 ☐	7:1—8:18 ☐
50	9:1—10:19 ☐	11:1—12:16 ☐	13:1—15:19 ☐	16:1—17:19 ☐	18:1—19:11 ☐	20:1-37 ☐	21:1—22:12 ☐
51	23:1—24:27 ☐	25:1—26:23 ☐	27:1—28:27 ☐	29:1-36 ☐	30:1—31:21 ☐	32:1-33 ☐	33:1—34:33 ☐
52	35:1—36:23 ☐	Ezra 1:1-11 ☐	2:1-70 ☐	3:1—4:24 ☐	5:1—6:22 ☐	7:1-28 ☐	8:1-36 ☐

Reading Schedule for the Recovery Version of the Old Testament with Footnotes

Wk.	Lord's Day	Monday	Tuesday	Wednesday	Thursday	Friday	Saturday
53	9:1—10:44 ☐	Neh. 1:1-11 ☐	2:1—3:32 ☐	4:1—5:19 ☐	6:1-19 ☐	7:1-73 ☐	8:1-18 ☐
54	9:1-20 ☐	9:21-38 ☐	10:1—11:36 ☐	12:1-47 ☐	13:1-31 ☐	Esth. 1:1-22 ☐	2:1—3:15 ☐
55	4:1—5:14 ☐	6:1—7:10 ☐	8:1-17 ☐	9:1—10:3 ☐	Job 1:1-22 ☐	2:1—3:26 ☐	4:1—5:27 ☐
56	6:1—7:21 ☐	8:1—9:35 ☐	10:1—11:20 ☐	12:1—13:28 ☐	14:1—15:35 ☐	16:1—17:16 ☐	18:1—19:29 ☐
57	20:1—21:34 ☐	22:1—23:17 ☐	24:1—25:6 ☐	26:1—27:23 ☐	28:1—29:25 ☐	30:1—31:40 ☐	32:1—33:33 ☐
58	34:1—35:16 ☐	36:1-33 ☐	37:1-24 ☐	38:1-41 ☐	39:1-30 ☐	40:1-24 ☐	41:1-34 ☐
59	42:1-17 ☐	Psa. 1:1-6 ☐	2:1—3:8 ☐	4:1—6:10 ☐	7:1—8:9 ☐	9:1—10:18 ☐	11:1—15:5 ☐
60	16:1—17:15 ☐	18:1-50 ☐	19:1—21:13 ☐	22:1-31 ☐	23:1—24:10 ☐	25:1—27:14 ☐	28:1—30:12 ☐
61	31:1—32:11 ☐	33:1—34:22 ☐	35:1—36:12 ☐	37:1-40 ☐	38:1—39:13 ☐	40:1—41:13 ☐	42:1—43:5 ☐
62	44:1-26 ☐	45:1-17 ☐	46:1—48:14 ☐	49:1—50:23 ☐	51:1—52:9 ☐	53:1—55:23 ☐	56:1—58:11 ☐
63	59:1—61:8 ☐	62:1—64:10 ☐	65:1—67:7 ☐	68:1-35 ☐	69:1—70:5 ☐	71:1—72:20 ☐	73:1—74:23 ☐
64	75:1—77:20 ☐	78:1-72 ☐	79:1—81:16 ☐	82:1—84:12 ☐	85:1—87:7 ☐	88:1—89:52 ☐	90:1—91:16 ☐
65	92:1—94:23 ☐	95:1—97:12 ☐	98:1—101:8 ☐	102:1—103:22 ☐	104:1—105:45 ☐	106:1-48 ☐	107:1-43 ☐
66	108:1—109:31 ☐	110:1—112:10 ☐	113:1—115:18 ☐	116:1—118:29 ☐	119:1-32 ☐	119:33-72 ☐	119:73-120 ☐
67	119:121-176 ☐	120:1—124:8 ☐	125:1—128:6 ☐	129:1—132:18 ☐	133:1—135:21 ☐	136:1—138:8 ☐	139:1—140:13 ☐
68	141:1—144:15 ☐	145:1—147:20 ☐	148:1—150:6 ☐	Prov. 1:1-33 ☐	2:1—3:35 ☐	4:1—5:23 ☐	6:1-35 ☐
69	7:1—8:36 ☐	9:1—10:32 ☐	11:1—12:28 ☐	13:1—14:35 ☐	15:1-33 ☐	16:1-33 ☐	17:1-28 ☐
70	18:1-24 ☐	19:1—20:30 ☐	21:1—22:29 ☐	23:1-35 ☐	24:1—25:28 ☐	26:1—27:27 ☐	28:1—29:27 ☐
71	30:1-33 ☐	31:1-31 ☐	Eccl. 1:1-18 ☐	2:1—3:22 ☐	4:1—5:20 ☐	6:1—7:29 ☐	8:1—9:18 ☐
72	10:1—11:10 ☐	12:1-14 ☐	S.S. 1:1-8 ☐	1:9-17 ☐	2:1-17 ☐	3:1-11 ☐	4:1-8 ☐
73	4:9-16 ☐	5:1-16 ☐	6:1-13 ☐	7:1-13 ☐	8:1-14 ☐	Isa. 1:1-11 ☐	1:12-31 ☐
74	2:1-22 ☐	3:1-26 ☐	4:1-6 ☐	5:1-30 ☐	6:1-13 ☐	7:1-25 ☐	8:1-22 ☐
75	9:1-21 ☐	10:1-34 ☐	11:1—12:6 ☐	13:1-22 ☐	14:1-14 ☐	14:15-32 ☐	15:1—16:14 ☐
76	17:1—18:7 ☐	19:1-25 ☐	20:1—21:17 ☐	22:1-25 ☐	23:1-18 ☐	24:1-23 ☐	25:1-12 ☐
77	26:1-:21 ☐	27:1-13 ☐	28:1-29 ☐	29:1-24 ☐	30:1-33 ☐	31:1—32:20 ☐	33:1-24 ☐
78	34:1-17 ☐	35:1-10 ☐	36:1-22 ☐	37:1-38 ☐	38:1—39:8 ☐	40:1-31 ☐	41:1-29 ☐

Reading Schedule for the Recovery Version of the Old Testament with Footnotes

Wk.	Lord's Day	Monday	Tuesday	Wednesday	Thursday	Friday	Saturday
79	42:1-25 ☐	43:1-28 ☐	44:1-28 ☐	45:1-25 ☐	46:1-13 ☐	47:1-15 ☐	48:1-22 ☐
80	49:1-13 ☐	49:14-26 ☐	50:1—51:23 ☐	52:1-15 ☐	53:1-12 ☐	54:1-17 ☐	55:1-13 ☐
81	56:1-12 ☐	57:1-21 ☐	58:1-14 ☐	59:1-21 ☐	60:1-22 ☐	61:1-11 ☐	62:1-12 ☐
82	63:1-19 ☐	64:1-12 ☐	65:1-25 ☐	66:1-24 ☐	Jer. 1:1-19 ☐	2:1-19 ☐	2:20-37 ☐
83	3:1-25 ☐	4:1-31 ☐	5:1-31 ☐	6:1-30 ☐	7:1-34 ☐	8:1-22 ☐	9:1-26 ☐
84	10:1-25 ☐	11:1—12:17 ☐	13:1-27 ☐	14:1-22 ☐	15:1-21 ☐	16:1—17:27 ☐	18:1-23 ☐
85	19:1—20:18 ☐	21:1—22:30 ☐	23:1-40 ☐	24:1—25:38 ☐	26:1—27:22 ☐	28:1—29:32 ☐	30:1-24 ☐
86	31:1-23 ☐	31:24-40 ☐	32:1-44 ☐	33:1-26 ☐	34:1-22 ☐	35:1-19 ☐	36:1-32 ☐
87	37:1-21 ☐	38:1-28 ☐	39:1—40:16 ☐	41:1—42:22 ☐	43:1—44:30 ☐	45:1—46:28 ☐	47:1—48:16 ☐
88	48:17-47 ☐	49:1-22 ☐	49:23-39 ☐	50:1-27 ☐	50:28-46 ☐	51:1-27 ☐	51:28-64 ☐
89	52:1-34 ☐	Lam. 1:1-22 ☐	2:1-22 ☐	3:1-39 ☐	3:40-66 ☐	4:1-22 ☐	5:1-22 ☐
90	Ezek. 1:1-14 ☐	1:15-28 ☐	2:1—3:27 ☐	4:1—5:17 ☐	6:1—7:27 ☐	8:1—9:11 ☐	10:1—11:25 ☐
91	12:1—13:23 ☐	14:1—15:8 ☐	16:1-63 ☐	17:1—18:32 ☐	19:1-14 ☐	20:1-49 ☐	21:1-32 ☐
92	22:1-31 ☐	23:1-49 ☐	24:1-27 ☐	25:1—26:21 ☐	27:1-36 ☐	28:1-26 ☐	29:1—30:26 ☐
93	31:1—32:32 ☐	33:1-33 ☐	34:1-31 ☐	35:1—36:21 ☐	36:22-38 ☐	37:1-28 ☐	38:1—39:29 ☐
94	40:1-27 ☐	40:28-49 ☐	41:1-26 ☐	42:1—43:27 ☐	44:1-31 ☐	45:1-25 ☐	46:1-24 ☐
95	47:1-23 ☐	48:1-35 ☐	Dan. 1:1-21 ☐	2:1-30 ☐	2:31-49 ☐	3:1-30 ☐	4:1-37 ☐
96	5:1-31 ☐	6:1-28 ☐	7:1-12 ☐	7:13-28 ☐	8:1-27 ☐	9:1-27 ☐	10:1-21 ☐
97	11:1-22 ☐	11:23-45 ☐	12:1-13 ☐	Hosea 1:1-11 ☐	2:1-23 ☐	3:1—4:19 ☐	5:1-15 ☐
98	6:1-11 ☐	7:1-16 ☐	8:1-14 ☐	9:1-17 ☐	10:1-15 ☐	11:1-12 ☐	12:1-14 ☐
99	13:1—14:9 ☐	Joel 1:1-20 ☐	2:1-16 ☐	2:17-32 ☐	3:1-21 ☐	Amos 1:1-15 ☐	2:1-16 ☐
100	3:1-15 ☐	4:1—5:27 ☐	6:1—7:17 ☐	8:1—9:15 ☐	Obad. 1-21 ☐	Jonah 1:1-17 ☐	2:1—4:11 ☐
101	Micah 1:1-16 ☐	2:1—3:12 ☐	4:1—5:15 ☐	6:1—7:20 ☐	Nahum 1:1-15 ☐	2:1—3:19 ☐	Hab. 1:1-17 ☐
102	2:1-20 ☐	3:1-19 ☐	Zeph. 1:1-18 ☐	2:1-15 ☐	3:1-20 ☐	Hag. 1:1-15 ☐	2:1-23 ☐
103	Zech. 1:1-21 ☐	2:1-13 ☐	3:1-10 ☐	4:1-14 ☐	5:1—6:15 ☐	7:1—8:23 ☐	9:1-17 ☐
104	10:1—11:17 ☐	12:1—13:9 ☐	14:1-21 ☐	Mal. 1:1-14 ☐	2:1-17 ☐	3:1-18 ☐	4:1-6 ☐

Reading Schedule for the Recovery Version of the New Testament with Footnotes

Wk.	Lord's Day	Monday	Tuesday	Wednesday	Thursday	Friday	Saturday
1	Matt. 1:1-2 ☐	1:3-7 ☐	1:8-17 ☐	1:18-25 ☐	2:1-23 ☐	3:1-6 ☐	3:7-17 ☐
2	4:1-11 ☐	4:12-25 ☐	5:1-4 ☐	5:5-12 ☐	5:13-20 ☐	5:21-26 ☐	5:27-48 ☐
3	6:1-8 ☐	6:9-18 ☐	6:19-34 ☐	7:1-12 ☐	7:13-29 ☐	8:1-13 ☐	8:14-22 ☐
4	8:23-34 ☐	9:1-13 ☐	9:14-17 ☐	9:18-34 ☐	9:35—10:5 ☐	10:6-25 ☐	10:26-42 ☐
5	11:1-15 ☐	11:16-30 ☐	12:1-14 ☐	12:15-32 ☐	12:33-42 ☐	12:43—13:2 ☐	13:3-12 ☐
6	13:13-30 ☐	13:31-43 ☐	13:44-58 ☐	14:1-13 ☐	14:14-21 ☐	14:22-36 ☐	15:1-20 ☐
7	15:21-31 ☐	15:32-39 ☐	16:1-12 ☐	16:13-20 ☐	16:21-28 ☐	17:1-13 ☐	17:14-27 ☐
8	18:1-14 ☐	18:15-22 ☐	18:23-35 ☐	19:1-15 ☐	19:16-30 ☐	20:1-16 ☐	20:17-34 ☐
9	21:1-11 ☐	21:12-22 ☐	21:23-32 ☐	21:33-46 ☐	22:1-22 ☐	22:23-33 ☐	22:34-46 ☐
10	23:1-12 ☐	23:13-39 ☐	24:1-14 ☐	24:15-31 ☐	24:32-51 ☐	25:1-13 ☐	25:14-30 ☐
11	25:31-46 ☐	26:1-16 ☐	26:17-35 ☐	26:36-46 ☐	26:47-64 ☐	26:65-75 ☐	27:1-26 ☐
12	27:27-44 ☐	27:45-56 ☐	27:57—28:15 ☐	28:16-20 ☐	Mark 1:1 ☐	1:2-6 ☐	1:7-13 ☐
13	1:14-28 ☐	1:29-45 ☐	2:1-12 ☐	2:13-28 ☐	3:1-19 ☐	3:20-35 ☐	4:1-25 ☐
14	4:26-41 ☐	5:1-20 ☐	5:21-43 ☐	6:1-29 ☐	6:30-56 ☐	7:1-23 ☐	7:24-37 ☐
15	8:1-26 ☐	8:27—9:1 ☐	9:2-29 ☐	9:30-50 ☐	10:1-16 ☐	10:17-34 ☐	10:35-52 ☐
16	11:1-16 ☐	11:17-33 ☐	12:1-27 ☐	12:28-44 ☐	13:1-13 ☐	13:14-37 ☐	14:1-26 ☐
17	14:27-52 ☐	14:53-72 ☐	15:1-15 ☐	15:16-47 ☐	16:1-8 ☐	16:9-20 ☐	Luke 1:1-4 ☐
18	1:5-25 ☐	1:26-46 ☐	1:47-56 ☐	1:57-80 ☐	2:1-8 ☐	2:9-20 ☐	2:21-39 ☐
19	2:40-52 ☐	3:1-20 ☐	3:21-38 ☐	4:1-13 ☐	4:14-30 ☐	4:31-44 ☐	5:1-26 ☐
20	5:27—6:16 ☐	6:17-38 ☐	6:39-49 ☐	7:1-17 ☐	7:18-23 ☐	7:24-35 ☐	7:36-50 ☐
21	8:1-15 ☐	8:16-25 ☐	8:26-39 ☐	8:40-56 ☐	9:1-17 ☐	9:18-26 ☐	9:27-36 ☐
22	9:37-50 ☐	9:51-62 ☐	10:1-11 ☐	10:12-24 ☐	10:25-37 ☐	10:38-42 ☐	11:1-13 ☐
23	11:14-26 ☐	11:27-36 ☐	11:37-54 ☐	12:1-12 ☐	12:13-21 ☐	12:22-34 ☐	12:35-48 ☐
24	12:49-59 ☐	13:1-9 ☐	13:10-17 ☐	13:18-30 ☐	13:31—14:6 ☐	14:7-14 ☐	14:15-24 ☐
25	14:25-35 ☐	15:1-10 ☐	15:11-21 ☐	15:22-32 ☐	16:1-13 ☐	16:14-22 ☐	16:23-31 ☐
26	17:1-19 ☐	17:20-37 ☐	18:1-14 ☐	18:15-30 ☐	18:31-43 ☐	19:1-10 ☐	19:11-27 ☐

Reading Schedule for the Recovery Version of the New Testament with Footnotes

Wk.	Lord's Day	Monday	Tuesday	Wednesday	Thursday	Friday	Saturday
27	Luke 19:28-48 ☐	20:1-19 ☐	20:20-38 ☐	20:39—21:4 ☐	21:5-27 ☐	21:28-38 ☐	22:1-20 ☐
28	22:21-38 ☐	22:39-54 ☐	22:55-71 ☐	23:1-43 ☐	23:44-56 ☐	24:1-12 ☐	24:13-35 ☐
29	24:36-53 ☐	John 1:1-13 ☐	1:14-18 ☐	1:19-34 ☐	1:35-51 ☐	2:1-11 ☐	2:12-22 ☐
30	2:23—3:13 ☐	3:14-21 ☐	3:22-36 ☐	4:1-14 ☐	4:15-26 ☐	4:27-42 ☐	4:43-54 ☐
31	5:1-16 ☐	5:17-30 ☐	5:31-47 ☐	6:1-15 ☐	6:16-31 ☐	6:32-51 ☐	6:52-71 ☐
32	7:1-9 ☐	7:10-24 ☐	7:25-36 ☐	7:37-52 ☐	7:53—8:11 ☐	8:12-27 ☐	8:28-44 ☐
33	8:45-59 ☐	9:1-13 ☐	9:14-34 ☐	9:35—10:9 ☐	10:10-30 ☐	10:31—11:4 ☐	11:5-22 ☐
34	11:23-40 ☐	11:41-57 ☐	12:1-11 ☐	12:12-24 ☐	12:25-36 ☐	12:37-50 ☐	13:1-11 ☐
35	13:12-30 ☐	13:31-38 ☐	14:1-6 ☐	14:7-20 ☐	14:21-31 ☐	15:1-11 ☐	15:12-27 ☐
36	16:1-15 ☐	16:16-33 ☐	17:1-5 ☐	17:6-13 ☐	17:14-24 ☐	17:25—18:11 ☐	18:12-27 ☐
37	18:28-40 ☐	19:1-16 ☐	19:17-30 ☐	19:31-42 ☐	20:1-13 ☐	20:14-18 ☐	20:19-22 ☐
38	20:23-31 ☐	21:1-14 ☐	21:15-22 ☐	21:23-25 ☐	Acts 1:1-8 ☐	1:9-14 ☐	1:15-26 ☐
39	2:1-13 ☐	2:14-21 ☐	2:22-36 ☐	2:37-41 ☐	2:42-47 ☐	3:1-18 ☐	3:19—4:22 ☐
40	4:23-37 ☐	5:1-16 ☐	5:17-32 ☐	5:33-42 ☐	6:1—7:1 ☐	7:2-29 ☐	7:30-60 ☐
41	8:1-13 ☐	8:14-25 ☐	8:26-40 ☐	9:1-19 ☐	9:20-43 ☐	10:1-16 ☐	10:17-33 ☐
42	10:34-48 ☐	11:1-18 ☐	11:19-30 ☐	12:1-25 ☐	13:1-12 ☐	13:13-43 ☐	13:44—14:5 ☐
43	14:6-28 ☐	15:1-12 ☐	15:13-34 ☐	15:35—16:5 ☐	16:6-18 ☐	16:19-40 ☐	17:1-18 ☐
44	17:19-34 ☐	18:1-17 ☐	18:18-28 ☐	19:1-20 ☐	19:21-41 ☐	20:1-12 ☐	20:13-38 ☐
45	21:1-14 ☐	21:15-26 ☐	21:27-40 ☐	22:1-21 ☐	22:22-29 ☐	22:30—23:11 ☐	23:12-15 ☐
46	23:16-30 ☐	23:31—24:21 ☐	24:22—25:5 ☐	25:6-27 ☐	26:1-13 ☐	26:14-32 ☐	27:1-26 ☐
47	27:27—28:10 ☐	28:11-22 ☐	28:23-31 ☐	Rom. 1:1-2 ☐	1:3-7 ☐	1:8-17 ☐	1:18-25 ☐
48	1:26—2:10 ☐	2:11-29 ☐	3:1-20 ☐	3:21-31 ☐	4:1-12 ☐	4:13-25 ☐	5:1-11 ☐
49	5:12-17 ☐	5:18—6:5 ☐	6:6-11 ☐	6:12-23 ☐	7:1-12 ☐	7:13-25 ☐	8:1-2 ☐
50	8:3-6 ☐	8:7-13 ☐	8:14-25 ☐	8:26-39 ☐	9:1-18 ☐	9:19—10:3 ☐	10:4-15 ☐
51	10:16—11:10 ☐	11:11-22 ☐	11:23-36 ☐	12:1-3 ☐	12:4-21 ☐	13:1-14 ☐	14:1-12 ☐
52	14:13-23 ☐	15:1-13 ☐	15:14-33 ☐	16:1-5 ☐	16:6-24 ☐	16:25-27 ☐	1 Cor. 1:1-4 ☐

Reading Schedule for the Recovery Version of the New Testament with Footnotes

Wk.	Lord's Day	Monday	Tuesday	Wednesday	Thursday	Friday	Saturday
53	1 Cor. 1:5-9 ☐	1:10-17 ☐	1:18-31 ☐	2:1-5 ☐	2:6-10 ☐	2:11-16 ☐	3:1-9 ☐
54	3:10-13 ☐	3:14-23 ☐	4:1-9 ☐	4:10-21 ☐	5:1-13 ☐	6:1-11 ☐	6:12-20 ☐
55	7:1-16 ☐	7:17-24 ☐	7:25-40 ☐	8:1-13 ☐	9:1-15 ☐	9:16-27 ☐	10:1-4 ☐
56	10:5-13 ☐	10:14-33 ☐	11:1-6 ☐	11:7-16 ☐	11:17-26 ☐	11:27-34 ☐	12:1-11 ☐
57	12:12-22 ☐	12:23-31 ☐	13:1-13 ☐	14:1-12 ☐	14:13-25 ☐	14:26-33 ☐	14:34-40 ☐
58	15:1-19 ☐	15:20-28 ☐	15:29-34 ☐	15:35-49 ☐	15:50-58 ☐	16:1-9 ☐	16:10-24 ☐
59	2 Cor. 1:1-4 ☐	1:5-14 ☐	1:15-22 ☐	1:23—2:11 ☐	2:12-17 ☐	3:1-6 ☐	3:7-11 ☐
60	3:12-18 ☐	4:1-6 ☐	4:7-12 ☐	4:13-18 ☐	5:1-8 ☐	5:9-15 ☐	5:16-21 ☐
61	6:1-13 ☐	6:14—7:4 ☐	7:5-16 ☐	8:1-15 ☐	8:16-24 ☐	9:1-15 ☐	10:1-6 ☐
62	10:7-18 ☐	11:1-15 ☐	11:16-33 ☐	12:1-10 ☐	12:11-21 ☐	13:1-10 ☐	13:11-14 ☐
63	Gal. 1:1-5 ☐	1:6-14 ☐	1:15-24 ☐	2:1-13 ☐	2:14-21 ☐	3:1-4 ☐	3:5-14 ☐
64	3:15-22 ☐	3:23-29 ☐	4:1-7 ☐	4:8-20 ☐	4:21-31 ☐	5:1-12 ☐	5:13-21 ☐
65	5:22-26 ☐	6:1-10 ☐	6:11-15 ☐	6:16-18 ☐	Eph. 1:1-3 ☐	1:4-6 ☐	1:7-10 ☐
66	1:11-14 ☐	1:15-18 ☐	1:19-23 ☐	2:1-5 ☐	2:6-10 ☐	2:11-14 ☐	2:15-18 ☐
67	2:19-22 ☐	3:1-7 ☐	3:8-13 ☐	3:14-18 ☐	3:19-21 ☐	4:1-4 ☐	4:5-10 ☐
68	4:11-16 ☐	4:17-24 ☐	4:25-32 ☐	5:1-10 ☐	5:11-21 ☐	5:22-26 ☐	5:27-33 ☐
69	6:1-9 ☐	6:10-14 ☐	6:15-18 ☐	6:19-24 ☐	Phil. 1:1-7 ☐	1:8-18 ☐	1:19-26 ☐
70	1:27—2:4 ☐	2:5-11 ☐	2:12-16 ☐	2:17-30 ☐	3:1-6 ☐	3:7-11 ☐	3:12-16 ☐
71	3:17-21 ☐	4:1-9 ☐	4:10-23 ☐	Col. 1:1-8 ☐	1:9-13 ☐	1:14-23 ☐	1:24-29 ☐
72	2:1-7 ☐	2:8-15 ☐	2:16-23 ☐	3:1-4 ☐	3:5-15 ☐	3:16-25 ☐	4:1-18 ☐
73	1 Thes. 1:1-3 ☐	1:4-10 ☐	2:1-12 ☐	2:13—3:5 ☐	3:6-13 ☐	4:1-10 ☐	4:11—5:11 ☐
74	5:12-28 ☐	2 Thes. 1:1-12 ☐	2:1-17 ☐	3:1-18 ☐	1 Tim. 1:1-2 ☐	1:3-4 ☐	1:5-14 ☐
75	1:15-20 ☐	2:1-7 ☐	2:8-15 ☐	3:1-13 ☐	3:14—4:5 ☐	4:6-16 ☐	5:1-25 ☐
76	6:1-10 ☐	6:11-21 ☐	2 Tim. 1:1-10 ☐	1:11-18 ☐	2:1-15 ☐	2:16-26 ☐	3:1-13 ☐
77	3:14—4:8 ☐	4:9-22 ☐	Titus 1:1-4 ☐	1:5-16 ☐	2:1-15 ☐	3:1-8 ☐	3:9-15 ☐
78	Philem. 1:1-11 ☐	1:12-25 ☐	Heb. 1:1-2 ☐	1:3-5 ☐	1:6-14 ☐	2:1-9 ☐	2:10-18 ☐

Reading Schedule for the Recovery Version of the New Testament with Footnotes

Wk.	Lord's Day	Monday	Tuesday	Wednesday	Thursday	Friday	Saturday
79	Heb. 3:1-6	3:7-19	4:1-9	4:10-13	4:14-16	5:1-10	5:11—6:3
80	6:4-8	6:9-20	7:1-10	7:11-28	8:1-6	8:7-13	9:1-4
81	9:5-14	9:15-28	10:1-18	10:19-28	10:29-39	11:1-6	11:7-19
82	11:20-31	11:32-40	12:1-2	12:3-13	12:14-17	12:18-26	12:27-29
83	13:1-7	13:8-12	13:13-15	13:16-25	James 1:1-8	1:9-18	1:19-27
84	2:1-13	2:14-26	3:1-18	4:1-10	4:11-17	5:1-12	5:13-20
85	1 Pet. 1:1-2	1:3-4	1:5	1:6-9	1:10-12	1:13-17	1:18-25
86	2:1-3	2:4-8	2:9-17	2:18-25	3:1-13	3:14-22	4:1-6
87	4:7-16	4:17-19	5:1-4	5:5-9	5:10-14	2 Pet. 1:1-2	1:3-4
88	1:5-8	1:9-11	1:12-18	1:19-21	2:1-3	2:4-11	2:12-22
89	3:1-6	3:7-9	3:10-12	3:13-15	3:16	3:17-18	1 John 1:1-2
90	1:3-4	1:5	1:6	1:7	1:8-10	2:1-2	2:3-11
91	2:12-14	2:15-19	2:20-23	2:24-27	2:28-29	3:1-5	3:6-10
92	3:11-18	3:19-24	4:1-6	4:7-11	4:12-15	4:16—5:3	5:4-13
93	5:14-17	5:18-21	2 John 1:1-3	1:4-9	1:10-13	3 John 1:1-6	1:7-14
94	Jude 1:1-4	1:5-10	1:11-19	1:20-25	Rev. 1:1-3	1:4-6	1:7-11
95	1:12-13	1:14-16	1:17-20	2:1-6	2:7	2:8-9	2:10-11
96	2:12-14	2:15-17	2:18-23	2:24-29	3:1-3	3:4-6	3:7-9
97	3:10-13	3:14-18	3:19-22	4:1-5	4:6-7	4:8-11	5:1-6
98	5:7-14	6:1-8	6:9-17	7:1-8	7:9-17	8:1-6	8:7-12
99	8:13—9:11	9:12-21	10:1-4	10:5-11	11:1-4	11:5-14	11:15-19
100	12:1-4	12:5-9	12:10-18	13:1-10	13:11-18	14:1-5	14:6-12
101	14:13-20	15:1-8	16:1-12	16:13-21	17:1-6	17:7-18	18:1-8
102	18:9—19:4	19:5-10	19:11-16	19:17-21	20:1-6	20:7-10	20:11-15
103	21:1	21:2	21:3-8	21:9-13	21:14-18	21:19-21	21:22-27
104	22:1	22:2	22:3-11	22:12-15	22:16-17	22:18-21	

Week 1 — Day 1

Dan. This matter is by the decree of the watch-
4:17 ers, and the decision is a command of the holy ones, to the intent that the living may know that the Most High is the Ruler over the kingdom of men and gives it to whomever He wills...

26 ...Your kingdom will be assured to you after you have come to know that the heavens do rule.

Date

Week 1 — Day 2

Rev. Immediately I was in spirit; and behold,
4:2 there was a throne set in heaven, and upon the throne *there was* One sitting.

11:15 And the seventh angel trumpeted; and there were loud voices in heaven, saying, The kingdom of the world has become the *kingdom* of our Lord and of His Christ, and He will reign forever and ever.

Date

Week 1 — Day 3

1 Pet. Blessed be the God and Father of our Lord
1:3 Jesus Christ, who according to His great mercy has regenerated us unto a living hope through the resurrection of Jesus Christ from the dead.

Gal. My children, with whom I travail again in
4:19 birth until Christ is formed in you.

Date

Week 1 — Day 4

Dan. I lifted up my eyes and I looked, and there
10:5-6 was a certain man, clothed in linen, whose loins were girded with the fine gold of Uphaz. His body also was like beryl, His face like the appearance of lightning, His eyes like torches of fire, His arms and His feet like the gleam of polished bronze, and the sound of His words like the sound of a multitude.

Date

Week 1 — Day 5

Dan. I watched until thrones were set, and the An-
7:9-10 cient of Days sat down. His clothing was like white snow, and the hair of His head was like pure wool; His throne was flames of fire, its wheels, burning fire. A stream of fire issued forth and came out from before Him. Thousands of thousands ministered to Him, and ten thousands of ten thousands stood before Him. The court of judgment sat, and the books were opened.

Date

Week 1 — Day 6

Dan. Then the iron, the clay, the bronze, the sil-
2:35 ver, and the gold were crushed all at once, and they became like chaff....And the stone that struck the image became a great mountain and filled the whole earth.

44 ...The God of the heavens will raise up a kingdom which will never be destroyed;... it will crush and put an end to all these kingdoms; and it will stand forever.

Date

Week 2 — Day 4

Today's verses

Dan. 9:2-3 In the first year of his reign I, Daniel, understood by means of the Scriptures the number of the years, which came as the word of Jehovah to Jeremiah the prophet, for the completion of the desolations of Jerusalem, *that is*, seventy years. So I set my face toward the Lord God to seek *Him* in prayer and supplications with fasting and sackcloth and ashes.

_____
Date

Week 2 — Day 5

Today's verses

Dan. 6:10 ...(In his upper room [Daniel] had windows open toward Jerusalem) and three times daily he knelt on his knees and prayed and gave thanks before his God, because he had *always* done so previously.

9:17 And now hear, O our God, the prayer of Your servant and his supplications, and cause Your face to shine upon Your sanctuary that has been desolated, for the Lord's sake.

_____
Date

Week 2 — Day 6

Today's verses

Dan. 3:17-18 ...Our God whom we serve is able to deliver us from the blazing furnace of fire, and He will deliver *us* out of your hand, O king. But if *He does* not, let it be known to you, O king, that we will not serve your gods nor worship the golden image that you have set up.

_____
Date

Week 2 — Day 1

Today's verses

Rev. 12:5 And she brought forth a son, a man-child, who is to shepherd all the nations with an iron rod; and her child was caught up to God and to His throne.

10-11 ...Now has come...the kingdom of our God and the authority of His Christ, for the accuser of our brothers has been cast down... And they overcame him...

_____
Date

Week 2 — Day 2

Today's verses

Dan. 1:8 But Daniel set his heart not to defile himself with the king's choice provision and with the wine that the king drank...

Rev. 2:13 I know where you dwell, where Satan's throne is; and you hold fast My name and have not denied My faith, even in the days of Antipas, My witness, My faithful one, who was killed among you, where Satan dwells.

_____
Date

Week 2 — Day 3

Today's verses

Exo. 4:14-16 ...Is there not Aaron your brother the Levite?...And even now he is coming out to meet you; and when he sees you, he will be glad in his heart. And you shall speak to him and put the words in his mouth, and I will be with your mouth and with his mouth, and will teach you what you shall do. And he shall speak for you to the people, and he shall be as a mouth for you, and you shall be as God to him.

_____
Date

Week 3 — Day 4

Today's verses

Dan. 2:34 You were watching until a stone was cut out without hands, and it struck the image at its feet of iron and clay and crushed them.

44 And in the days of those kings the God of the heavens will raise up a kingdom which will never be destroyed;...it will crush and put an end to all these kingdoms; and it will stand forever.

_____
Date

Week 3 — Day 5

Today's verses

Dan. 2:35 ...And the stone that struck the image became a great mountain and filled the whole earth.

45 Inasmuch as you saw that out of the mountain a stone was cut without hands and that it crushed the iron, the bronze, the clay, the silver, and the gold, the great God has made known to the king what will happen afterward...

_____
Date

Week 3 — Day 6

Today's verses

Dan. 7:13-14 I watched in the night visions, and there with the clouds of heaven One like a Son of Man was coming; and He came to the Ancient of Days, and they brought Him near before Him. And to Him was given dominion, glory, and a kingdom, that all the peoples, nations, and languages might serve Him. His dominion is an eternal dominion, which will not pass away; and His kingdom is one that will not be destroyed.

_____
Date

Week 3 — Day 1

Today's verses

Dan. 2:28 But there is a God in the heavens who reveals mysteries, and He has made known to King Nebuchadnezzar what will happen in the last days. This is your dream, even the visions of your head upon your bed.

31-32 You, O king, were watching, and there was a single great image. This image, large and its brightness surpassing, stood opposite you; and its appearance was frightful. Concerning this image, its head was of fine gold...

_____
Date

Week 3 — Day 2

Today's verses

Dan. 2:32-33 Concerning this image, its head was of fine gold, its breast and its arms of silver, its abdomen and its thighs of bronze, its legs of iron, its feet partly of iron and partly of clay.

7:12 And as for the rest of the beasts, their dominion was taken away, but an extension of life was given to them for a season and a time.

_____
Date

Week 3 — Day 3

Today's verses

Dan. 7:7 ...There was a fourth beast, dreadful and frightful and exceedingly strong;...and it was different from all the beasts that were before it; and it had ten horns.

Rev. 17:11-12 And the beast who was and is not, he himself is also the eighth and is out of the seven....And the ten horns which you saw are ten kings, who...receive authority as kings for one hour with the beast.

_____
Date

Week 4 — Day 4	Today's verses	Week 4 — Day 5	Today's verses	Week 4 — Day 6	Today's verses
Heb. 11:1	Now faith is the substantiation of things hoped for, the conviction of things not seen.	2 Pet. 1:19	And we have the prophetic word *made* more firm, to which you do well to give heed as to a lamp shining in a dark place, until the day dawns and the morning star rises in your hearts.	Rev. 3:10	Because you have kept the word of My endurance, I also will keep you out of the hour of trial...
Eph. 6:19	And for me, that utterance may be given to me in the opening of my mouth, to make known in boldness the mystery of the gospel.	Matt. 24:42	Watch therefore, for you do not know on what day your Lord comes.	2 Tim. 4:8	Henceforth there is laid up for me the crown of righteousness, with which the Lord, the righteous Judge, will recompense me in that day; and not only me but also all those who have loved His appearing.

Date — *Date* — *Date*

Week 4 — Day 1	Today's verses	Week 4 — Day 2	Today's verses	Week 4 — Day 3	Today's verses
Dan. 9:2	...I, Daniel, understood by means of the Scriptures the number of the years...for the completion of the desolations of Jerusalem, *that is*, seventy years.	Dan. 9:26-27	And after the sixty-two weeks Messiah will be cut off:...and the people of the prince who will come will destroy the city and the sanctuary....And he will make a firm covenant with the many for one week; and in the middle of the week he will cause the sacrifice and the oblation to cease and will replace the sacrifice and the oblation with abominations of the desolator...	Col. 2:2	...Being knit together in love and unto all the riches of the full assurance of understanding, unto the full knowledge of the mystery of God, Christ.
	24 Seventy weeks are apportioned for your people and for your holy city, to close the transgression, and to make an end of sins, and to make propitiation for iniquity, and to bring in the righteousness of the ages, and to seal up vision and prophet, and to anoint the Holy of Holies.			Eph. 3:4, 6	By which, in reading *it*, you can perceive my understanding in the mystery of Christ,...that in Christ Jesus the Gentiles are fellow heirs and fellow members of the Body and fellow partakers of the promise through the gospel.

Date — *Date* — *Date*

Week 5 — Day 4   Today's verses

Eph. For our wrestling is not against blood and
6:12 flesh but against the rulers, against the authorities, against the world-rulers of this darkness, against the spiritual *forces* of evil in the heavenlies.

Matt. ...If I, by the Spirit of God, cast out the de-
12:28-29 mons, then the kingdom of God has come upon you. Or how can anyone enter into the house of the strong man and plunder his goods unless he first binds the strong man?...

_____
Date

Week 5 — Day 5   Today's verses

Psa. Let the faithful ones exult in glory; let them
149:5-6 give a ringing shout upon their beds. Let the high praises of God be in their throats, and a two-edged sword in their hand.

9 To execute upon them the judgment written. This honor is for all His faithful ones. Hallelujah!

_____
Date

Week 5 — Day 6   Today's verses

Col. Who delivered us out of the authority of dark-
1:13 ness and transferred *us* into the kingdom of the Son of His love.

Dan. And the kingdom and dominion and the
7:27 greatness of the kingdoms under the whole heaven will be given to the people of the saints of the Most High; His kingdom is an eternal kingdom...

_____
Date

Week 5 — Day 1   Today's verses

Dan. I watched until thrones were set, and the An-
7:9-10 cient of Days sat down....His throne was flames of fire, its wheels, burning fire. A stream of fire issued forth and came out from before Him. Thousands of thousands ministered to Him, and ten thousands of ten thousands stood before Him. The court of judgment sat, and the books were opened.

_____
Date

Week 5 — Day 2   Today's verses

Dan. I watched in the night visions, and there with
7:13-14 the clouds of heaven One like a Son of Man was coming; and He came to the Ancient of Days, and they brought Him near before Him. And to Him was given dominion, glory, and a kingdom, that all the peoples, nations, and languages might serve Him. His dominion is an eternal dominion, which will not pass away; and His kingdom is one that will not be destroyed.

_____
Date

Week 5 — Day 3   Today's verses

Eph. Put on the whole armor of God that you
6:11 may be able to stand against the stratagems of the devil.

Rev. ...Now has come the salvation and the power
12:10 and the kingdom of our God and the authority of His Christ, for the accuser of our brothers has been cast down, who accuses them before our God day and night.

_____
Date

Week 6 — Day 4	Today's verses	Week 6 — Day 5	Today's verses	Week 6 — Day 6	Today's verses

Week 6 — Day 4 — Today's verses

Dan. 3:17-18 ...Our God whom we serve is able to deliver us from the blazing furnace of fire, and He will deliver us out of your hand....But if *He does* not, let it be known to you, O king, that we will not serve your gods nor worship the golden image that you have set up.

25 ...Look, I see four men loose, walking in the midst of the fire; and they are not harmed. And the appearance of the fourth is like a son of the gods.

Date

Week 6 — Day 5 — Today's verses

Dan. 4:37 Now I, Nebuchadnezzar, praise and exalt and honor the King of the heavens, because all His works are truth and His ways justice, and because He is able to abase those who walk in pride.

5:22-23 And you his descendant, Belshazzar,...have brought the vessels of His house before you,...and you have praised the gods,...which do not see nor hear nor know. But the God in whose hand is your breath and to whom all your ways *belong*, you have not honored.

Date

Week 6 — Day 6 — Today's verses

Dan. 6:10-11 Now when Daniel came to know that the writing had been signed, he went to his house (in his upper room he had windows open toward Jerusalem) and three times daily he knelt on his knees and prayed and gave thanks before his God, because he had *always* done so previously. Then these men assembled and found Daniel making petition and supplication before his God.

Week 6 — Day 1 — Today's verses

Dan. 12:3 And those who have insight will shine like the shining of the heavenly expanse, and those who turn many to righteousness, like the stars, forever and ever.

Rev. 1:20 The mystery of the seven stars which you saw upon My right hand and the seven golden lampstands: The seven stars are the messengers of the seven churches, and the seven lampstands are the seven churches.

Date

Week 6 — Day 2 — Today's verses

2 Pet. 1:19 And we have the prophetic word *made* more firm, to which you do well to give heed as to a lamp shining in a dark place, until the day dawns and the morning star rises in your hearts.

Rev. 3:1 And to the messenger of the church in Sardis write: These things says He who has the seven Spirits of God and the seven stars: I know your works, that you are living, and yet you are dead.

Date

Week 6 — Day 3 — Today's verses

Dan. 1:8 But Daniel set his heart not to defile himself with the king's choice provision...

16 Therefore the steward withheld their *portion of* the choice provision and the wine that they were to drink and gave them vegetables.

2:17 Then Daniel went to his house and made the thing known to Hananiah, Mishael, and Azariah, his companions.

Date